PRINCETON THEOLOGICAL MONOGRAPH SERIES

Dikran Y. Hadidian

General Editor

19

THE THEOLOGY OF ELECTRICITY

FRIEDRICH CHRISTOPH OETINGER, One of the
noted "electrical theologians" of the 18th century.

THE
THEOLOGY
OF
ELECTRICITY

On the Encounter and Explanation
of Theology and Science in the
17th and 18th Centuries

by
Ernst Benz

Translated
by Wolfgang Taraba

Edited and with an Introduction
by Dennis Stillings

PICKWICK PUBLICATIONS
Allison Park, Pennsylvania

Originally published as *Theologie der Elektrizität. Zur Begegnung und Auseinandersetzung von Theologie und Naturwissenschaft im 17. und 18. Jahrhundert von Ernst Benz,* published by Verlag der Akademie der Wissenschaften und der Literatur, Mainz, 1970.

Published by Pickwick Publications
4137 Timberlane Drive, Allison Park, PA 15101-2932

Printed in the United States of America

Library of Congress Cataloging-in-Publications Data

Benz, Ernst, 1907-
    [Theologie der Elektrizität, English]
    The theology of electricity : on the encounter and explanation of theology and science in the 17th and 18th centuries / by Ernst Benz ; translated by Wolfgang Taraba ; edited and with an introduction by Dennis Stillings.
    p. cm. -- (Princeton theological monograph series ; 19)
    Translation of : Theologie der Elektrizität.
    ISBN 0-915138-92-1
    1. Electricity–Religious aspects–Christianity–History of doctrines–17th century. 2. Magnetism–Religious aspects–Christianity–History of doctrines–17th century. 3. Electricity–Religious aspects–Christianity–History of doctrines–18th century. 4. Magnetism–Religious aspects–Christianity--History of doctrines–18th century. I. Title. II. Series.
BL265.E6B4613 1989
215'.3--dc20
                                  89-28664
                                    CIP

Contents

ATHANASIUS KIRCHER, *Magnes sive primus artis*
bk. 3, *Artis, magneticae mundus sive catena magnetica*
(1643), which treats of the magnetic force of the earth.
The frontispiece depicts the double-headed eagle
electrified and magnetized.

Editor's Preface

In 1968, I was working as a research librarian at Medtronic, Inc., a major manufacturer of medical devices, in particular the implantable cardiac pacemaker. Late in that year, Earl Bakken, founder of Medtronic, approached me about a special project–he wanted me to collect the history of bioelectricity and electromedicine, in the form of printed materials and original apparatus. This project eventually led to the establishment of The Bakken: A Library and Museum of Electricity in Life, which currently houses some 12,000 publications and 2000 artifacts on these subjects.

Ironically, before I took on this project, I had no interest at all in electricity and the physics of it. I was immersed in German studies in graduate school, where I was mostly interested in applying the methods of Jung's analytical psychology to the interpretation of literature, and I was teaching 18th-century humanities. It was through C. G. Jung's work, especially his *Psychology and Alchemy*, that I came to develop an interest in the history of electricity since, through Jung, I was able to see that much of the imagery and nomenclature of alchemy had been transferred, virtually unchanged, into the speculations of the new electrical science of the 18th century. When I perceived this, I was able to trace the myths, metaphors, and archetypal images that permeated 18th-century electrical thinking back to alchemical and to certain Gnostic writings.

In 1972, I presented a paper at the 24th International Conference of the History of Medicine in which I emphasized some of the ancient images and ideas that led to the association of the cardiovascular system with electrical activity. After my lecture, a number of people approached me and asked if I knew of the recently published work by Ernst Benz, the *Theologie der Elektrizität*. I had not yet heard of the book, but said I would get a copy as soon as possible. A couple of years went by before I finally received a copy through a foreign book search service. A brief glance at the contents of the book made me very excited: it looked as though Benz was the only other person beside myself who had perceived the hermetic background of electrical philosophizing. I soon commissioned Wolfgang Taraba to do this translation.

Benz's Program

Benz's main program in *Theology of Electricity* is to concern himself with the "interrelationship of the religious and scientific consciousness." More specifically, Benz intends to establish the claim that the "discovery of electricity and the simultaneous discovery of magnetic and galvanic phenomena were accompanied by a most significant change in the image of God." Furthermore, Benz claims that these discoveries led to a "completely new understanding of the relation of body and soul, of spirit and matter . . ." (p. 2).

Benz illustrates his concern with the traditional split between science and religion by juxtaposing the personalities and perceptions of Franklin and Mesmer. In terms of Jungian typology, the former might be said to represent the archetypal American extravert, the empiricist and practical manipulator of the external world. Mesmer, on the other hand, is portrayed as operating within the realms of intuition and feeling, ill adapted to the practicalities of making his methods acceptable to the powers-that-be; he is tuned to cosmic feeling, which empathizes with the workings of nature, and which in turn is abstracted from nature and safely ordered within a metaphysical system. Franklin might argue that a ball is spherical, hard, and suitable for a number of uses; Mesmer that it is gold-colored, round, and therefore a symbol of cosmic wholeness. This argument, suitably expanded and generalized, lies close to the heart of the persistent opposition between science and religion–Franklin's side giving dominant value to the objects of external reality; Mesmer's, to the inner states evoked by the object.

Benz looks forward to the time when religion and science will resolve their apparent differences. He sees the effect of the "electrical theologians" as demonstrating that science and religion do motivate each other, and it is important that we examine a few of the themes that demonstrate this process.

Benz and the History of Electromedicine and Bioelectricity

Electrical and magnetic phenomena have been associated with ideas of the soul, with divine judgment, and with psychic matters, from the beginnings of recorded history and probably before. The thunderbolts of Zeus were cast down upon those who offended him. Amber and other electrics were perceived as having a kind of "soul." Ancient Sumerians wore magnetic amulets engraved with images of Marduk[1]–

He Who Causes Action at a Distance—to ward off those evil spirits that gave rise to specific diseases. It is possible that primitive peoples used pools of electric fish (the Mediterranean torpedo and Nile catfish) for purposes of exorcising spirits by means of subconvulsive electroshock therapy.[2] In fact, electroexorcism was used by J. Priestley (1733-1804),[3] a theologian and also the first historian of electricity. This peculiar therapy has been practiced down into our own century.[4]

Medical applications of the discharge of electric fish for treatment of headache, arthritis, and anal prolapse were recorded by Scribonius Largus[5] and Dioscorides[6] in the second century A.D. The electrical discharge of the live Mediterranean torpedo was used by Dawud al Antaki in the 16th century for the treatment of epilepsy.[7]

By the time of Harvey and Gilbert, the role of electricity and/or magnetism in the physiological functioning of the body was already a matter of wide speculation.[8] By the mid-18th century, it was assumed by many prominent physicians and physiologists that electricity was indeed intrinsic to the life processes of both animals and humans.[9] The Galvani-Volta controversy,[10] and many French experiments on the applications of electrical current to freshly decapitated corpses,[11] made it appear quite plausible that electricity *was* the vital fluid, and that its proper application could raise even the dead. The great Frankenstein myth, perceived and recorded by Mary Shelley in her book, *Frankenstein; or, The Modern Prometheus*[12] was not the imaginative flight of fancy one might at first think. At that time, electrical resurrection was probably considered, from the scientific point of view, not much more than a short-term extrapolation from what was then known about bioelectrical effects. Considering this history, it is small wonder that electricity was brought under theological scrutiny. Even as late as the 1930s, Albert S. Hyman, a New York physician who developed an early version of the artificial cardiac pacemaker, was attacked by religious proponents for interfering with the divine will[13] —a judgment curiously reserved for electrical physicians, since it can be argued on this basis that a wide variety of other medical interventions do the same.

Benz has been criticized for his statement (p. 15) that electrical and magnetic phenomena had not been adequately distinguished from one another by the time of Kircher (1602-1680). Even though a number of early investigators had noted the difference between the effects of amber and lodestone, and even though the great Gilbert, in his classic treatise *De Magnete*,[14] had clearly distinguished among electrical and magnetic effects, confusion persisted. Even in the late

18th century, learned disquisitions[15] addressed these distinctions, and even those between magnetism, electricity, and animal magnetism, as though these were still live topics. It appears safe to assume that the "nonspecialist" of that era was not yet completely clear about the differences. In any case, this "error" on Benz's part has no real bearing on the argument. Indeed, one could say that subsequent experimentation by Oersted, Faraday, and others–showing the intimate relation between electricity and magnetism–would have resulted in even richer metaphysical and theological speculation.

Benz is also incorrect in stating that the only means for generating "low voltage" prior to the invention of the Leyden jar (in 1744) was the electric "log" or "wand"–a glass tube set into a wooden handle, which was then rubbed with cat's fur or silk. There were, in fact, several elaborate electrostatic generators in existence before 1744, capable of producing several thousand volts, but with a very small current. (Benz also confuses electrical potential [volts] with electrical current [amps]. The Leyden jar was the first artificial device for producing large currents.)

One more small point of criticism should be made here. Contrary to Benz's evaluation, glass harmonicas, modeled after Franklin's design, need not take a back seat, in terms of tonal quality, to the instruments of Kircher and Mesmer. (see pp. 16f.)

Alchemy Divides and Conquers

As I collected early 18th-century writings on electricity, it soon became clear to me that a great deal of symbolism, and even the nomenclature, of alchemy had been carried over into the new electrical theorizing. Merely scanning the titles of early books on electricity confirms this. Electricity is the "ethereal fire," the "desideratum," the "quintessential fire"–all expressions that would be familiar to an alchemist. For the early electrotherapist, electricity was the *medicina catholica*, the "cheap thing to be found everywhere"; it was the long-sought panacea. This belief was clearly reflected in the utterly promiscuous use of electricity in the treatment of disease. This archetypally based belief continues to be asserted in modern claims by quacks–and occasionally by serious medical practitioners–for the extraordinary unrecognized medical value of electricity, magnetism, and electromagnetic waves.

Electricity was the last of the classical sciences to be born at the time when the rule of the materialistic, mechanistic view of nature was gathering full steam, and it emerged as a sort of medical/spiritual "fifth column" within the body of an otherwise generally mechanistic science and medicine. In physiology, even at the present time, chemical factors are emphasized over the accompanying electrical events. This emphasis is made with an insistence that makes one suspicious that bio-electricity still raises the spectre of vitalism among physiologists and biochemists. According to Robert O. Becker and Andrew A. Marino:

> Practically from the time of its discovery, electromagnetic energy was identified by the vitalists as being the "life force," and consequently it has occupied a central position in the conflict between [mechanism and vitalism] for the past three centuries. While the modern view of the role of electromagnetic energy in life processes is not that of the mysterious force of the vitalists, it has nevertheless inherited the emotional and dogmatic aspects of the earlier conflict.[16]

Electricity also still evokes, on an unconscious level, images of that paradoxical figure of alchemy, Mercurius, and of the elusive vital fluid that transcends the merely mechanical. Indeed, the strange paradoxes of modern quantum mechanics and the endless popular speculations on the role of consciousness in the material world, not to mention the actual transmutations of metals now possible, seem to be outward manifestations of the symbols that drove alchemy and now drive modern physics.

But alchemy was fundamentally a *monstrum compositum*, an illegitimate or, more precisely, a *premature* intuitive expression of underlying symbols hopelessly enmeshed within an undiscriminated mixture of psyche and substance. After centuries of concern chiefly for otherworldly things, the world and the matter of which it is constituted had become, for the Western man of the 15th century, a great *fascinosum*–a fascination that would extend down to the present day. The 15th-century voyages of exploration and the golden age of alchemy therefore coincide. At first matter was a great mystery, a vacuum of knowledge that drew into itself the projections of the structure and dynamics of the human psyche. Mind became intimately bound up with matter, and this condition was expressed in the obscure symbolism of alchemical formulae. With the beginnings of modern chemistry and physics, alchemy split into two directions: one was that of mainstream science and technology, the other, by a more subterranean and quiet path, led toward the development of psychology and the discovery of the unconscious. Electricity, expressing both material and immaterial effects, was not readily divested of the ancient symbolic projections; hence, by its ambiguous and paradoxical nature, it brought philosophers into yet closer contact with the unconscious. On the other hand, material science could not pull itself clear from the psychological residuum that adhered to electrical theorizing, thus permitting the symbols carried by electricity to drive modern science toward accomplishments that strongly echo the goals of alchemy: the transmutation and spiritualization of matter.

The lack of a concept of the unconscious, the failure to actually achieve the transmutation of metals, and the rise and success of mechanistic science, all hastened the demise of alchemy. But with the splitting-off of alchemy into an exoteric "alchemy of matter"–i.e., normal chemistry and physics–the psychic residuum made it possible for an intuitive perception of the existence of the unconscious psyche to arise.

While Benz draws very little attention to this aspect of his account of the electrical theology, his detailed and conscientious exposition of the thoughts of the electrical theologians provides important clues leading toward an understanding of this important historical transformation of consciousness.

The Electrical Unconscious

An examination of how the electrical theologians conceived of the role of that primordial light, electricity, reveals how close they were able to come to the beginnings of a psychology of the unconscious. For the electrical theologians, there is not only a "conscious and rational" life, but a "sensory, growth-like, sensitive" life. This "sensuous soul" (the unconscious) is electric, and is nourished by the "electrical fire" (read "libido" or "psychic energy"). Man is a being "involved in all levels of life–the material, vegetable, animal." His soul "has deep roots in pre-human realms." Man's spiritual life is rooted "in the organic structures and physico-chemical processes of his bodily existence." Not only is the "animalistic" soul the "nourishment of the rational soul," but the rational soul "needs this substratum in order to function." The two should generate thoughts that stand in opposition to one another. (One is reminded of Goethe's "Two souls, alas, do dwell within my breast.")[17] And in a clear prefiguration of Jung's conceptions of the effects of complexes and archetypes, Oetinger says that the images that arise out of the "animalistic soul" must be overcome by conscious reflection or meditation, lest "you [be] forced to act according to the needs of the body." The texts that Benz examines seem not only to refer to the fact of a conscious and unconscious mind, but to address the more dynamic functions of archetypal possession, the compensatory function of the unconscious, and the drive toward individuation as freedom from the opposites.

Apocatastasis

Benz emphasizes the apocatastatic themes of revelation, restitution, and final judgment as interpreted through Oetinger's electrical theology. Oetinger believes that the electrical theologians are rediscovering the magic of the ancients–that science and technology are mere reconstructions of this ancient wisdom. The electrical theologians are therefore bringing about the restitution of the central magic and meaning of the world at the end of time. In fact, Oetinger uses a line of thought very similar to the one we have used here in discussing the prefigurative aspects of alchemy with regard to the development of microphysics and a psychology of the unconscious. Unfortunately, Oetinger concretizes this "lost wisdom," as though it once existed in some rational form when, in fact, it existed as sets of symbols, images, and metaphors, many of which still remain to be understood–just as was the case with the ostensibly bizarre imagery of alchemy.[18] The recovery of this lost wisdom will shortly precede the return of the Kingdom of God.

Apocatastatic and apocalyptic ideas associated with science should not be viewed as a peculiarity of an obscure theology of the 18th century. What was then discussed in open terms now appears to unconsciously order the content and structure of modern scientific speculation. "Closure" theories of the cosmos abound: we hear of neutron-proton ratios and their relationship to the eventual collapse of the universe; superstring theory and the new Theories of Everything are clearly apocatastatic. Dark Matter is envisioned as a godlike threatening aspect of the unknown universe; an eternally menacing "Nemesis planet" that directs consmic debris toward earth is hypothesized. Other technologies, such as the undersea robot, "Alvin," for deep-sea scanning, and LandSat analyses of the earth's surface and what lies immediately beneath it, seem designed to effect–at least in the imagery of our expectations–a revelation of all things at the end of time.[19]

DENNIS STILLINGS
Minneapolis, Minnesota
June 1989

NOTES

1. Two examples of these, once in the Editor's collection, are now in the Bakken Library.

2. Peter Kellaway, "The Part Played by Electric Fish in the Early History of Bio-electricity and Electrotherapy," *Bulletin of the History of Medicine* 20 (1946): 112.

3. *The Dictionary of National Biography*, vol. XVI, repr. (Oxford, 1967-1968), p. 360.

4. See Carl A. Wickland, *Thirty Years Among the Dead* (London, 1968). This book was first published in 1924.

5. *De compositionibus medicamentorum. Liber unus, antehac nusquam excusus: Joanne Ruellio* (Paris, 1528).

6. Pedanius Dioscorides of Anazarbos, *The Greek Herbal of Dioscorides, illustrated by a Byzantine A.D. 512, Englished by John Goodyer A.D. 1655* (London, 1968). Facsimile of 1934 edition.

7. J. O. Leibowitz, "Electroshock Therapy in Ibn-Sina's Canon," *Journal of the History of Medicine* 12 (1957): 71.

8. See Dennis Stillings, "Early Attempts at Electrical Control of the Heart: Harvey to Hyman," *Acta Congressus Internationalis XXIV Historiae Artis Medicinae* (Budapest, 1976).; *Artifex* 5,3 (June 1986): 1.

9. H. E. Hoff, "Galvani and the Pre-Galvanian Electrophysiologists," *Annals of Science* 1 (1936): 157.

10. Bern Dibner, *Galvani-Volta* (Norwalk, Conn., 1952).

11. Since most of these experiments were carried out in France during the Revolution, there was no shortage of such material.

12. London, 1818.

13. D. C. Schechter, *Background of Clinical Cardiac Electrostimulation,* pt. V: "Direct Electrostimulation of Heart without Thoracotomy" (Minneapolis, [n.d.]): 612.

14. *De magnete, magneticisque corporibus, et de magno magnete tellure; physiologia nova* (London, 1600).

15. For example, Jan Hendrik van Swinden's (1746-1823) *Recueil de Mémoires sur l'Analogie de l'Électricité et du Magnétisme* . . . . (Le Haye, 1784).

16. *Electromagnetism and Life* (Albany, 1982), p. 4.

17. St. Paul's version of this idea is to be found in Romans 7:19-20: "For the good that I would I do not: but the evil which I would not, that I do. Now if I do that I would not, it is no more I that do it, but sin that dwelleth within me."

18. Jung revealed much of the meaning hidden within the symbolism of alchemy. His discussion of the meaning of fire in alchemy—too extensive to attend to here—adds considerable support to the alchemy-rooted images connected to the nascent electrical science.

19. See Stillings, "Meditations on the Atom and Time: An Attempt to Define the Imagery of War and Death in the Late Twentieth Century," *ARCHAEUS* 4 (1986); "Invasion of the Archetypes," *Gnosis* 10 (Winter 1989); and "The World Will End in 2010," *Critique* 31 (June/July/Aug/Sept. 1989).

Translator's Note

Popular wisdom holds that—since both German and English belong to the Indo-European family of languages—there is a decided advantage for Germans in learning English and for the native speaker of English in tackling German. While this is true on the level of basic vocabularies where cognates abound, this widely held belief becomes problematic when we compare the characteristics of English syntax with that of German: the involved and lengthy dependent clauses, which German authors are so fond of, frequently offer great difficulty to speakers of English. The fact that German puts the conjugated verb at the end of the dependent clause, has bewildered critics of German from the beginning students of the language to such celebrities as Mark Twain. And this is not the only difficulty posed by the language.

When dealing with highly specialized texts in the fields of philosophy and theology, despair is not uncommon even among readers who may feel quite at home understanding the meaning of less demanding works in the target language. What *are* the proper English terms for such words as *Geist* or *Wesen*? Dictionaries are of but limited help. We have to spend a great deal of thought and use our intuition to come up with an acceptable translation of these and other terms from the respective context in which they appear. And thus—in the case of *Geist*, for example—we may have to render the German word in any one of the following ways: "spirit," "intellect," "mind," "wit," "genius," "ghost," "specter," "apparition," "phantom," "sprite," or even "demon."

In my translation of Ernst Benz's *Theologie der Elektricität,* I have attempted to come as close as possible to the author's intended meaning. How well I have succeeded in this is up to the reader to judge. Every translation is also an interpretation and, thus, ultimately subjective.

Another matter of considerable concern to the translator is the *style* of his author. What liberties is he entitled to take? Should he make three or four sentences out of one sentence, which runs nine or ten printed lines long in the original? This may seem advisable, at least for the sake of clarity. Or should he preserve the "flavor" of the author's style and refrain from doing so? In most cases, when faced with such a decision, I have opted for the latter choice. Should this have resulted in "wooden" English, I apologize.

I want to conclude with a quotation from Friedrich Nietzsche, one of the few great stylists in German, who laments: "What torture books written in Germaan are for anyone who has a *third* ear! How vexed one stands before the slowly revolving swamp of sounds that do not sound like anything and rhythms that do not dance, called a 'book' among the Germans!"* Ernst Benz's *Theologie der Elektrizität,* viewed from a Nietzschean perspective, is a typically *German* work in its inspiring as well as in its discouraging aspects: it is eminently deep and rewarding to the reader, but its meaning is occasionally hard to grasp.

WOLFGANG TARABA
University of Minnesota

* *Beyond Good and Evil,* with commentary by Walter Kaufmann (New York: Vintage Books/ Random House, 1966), p. 182.

Acknowledgment

This translation was made possible by a grant from The Bakken: A Library and Museum of Electricity in Life. The Bakken is located in Minneapolis, Minn., and houses a library of some 12,000 volumes of original works and secondary literature relating directly or indirectly to the theme of electromedicine, bioelectricity, magnetotherapy, and bioelectromagnetics. These works date from the 13th century. In addition, the collections include some 3000 artifacts and original instruments, including Sumerian magnetite cylinder seals, ancient representations of electric fish, scores of original electrical machines from the 18th and 19th centuries and a large collection of manuscripts, ephemera, and illustrative material. Many of the works cited in the Editor's Preface are in the Bakken collection.

Introduction

     In view of the present *niveau* of theology and the sciences, my topic *The Theology of Electricity and Magnetism* creates the impression of containing an element of the ludicrous. The respective views and methods of theology and the sciences have had such divergent developments since the middle of the last century and have so deliberately kept apart fron each other that it may appear odd to ignore this separation and relate each of these two fields of knowledge directly to the other. Even a strictly historical approach to such a fusing together of theology and the sciences holds but little promise to the prevalent modern view–the research of 18th-century physico-theologians is considered superannuated and their scientific ideas are regarded as being just as antiquated as their theology. Actually, modern historical research in the humanities and in theology hardly pays any attention to the cosmology and natural theology of the 18th century.[1] Modern theology has reduced the religious problem to asking questions about the personal relationship between man and God, questions regarding the function of belief, and it has almost completely neglected the theological aspects of cosmology, of natural theology, of man's place in the universe and in the chain of other living forms in our world. On the other hand, in their positivistic concept of scholarship, the natural sciences have consciously abrogated their earlier ties to a theological world view, and they now base their scholarly ethos on the refusal to pose any speculative, metaphysical questions.

     This contemporary situation–characterized by most theologians and scientists–as being the best of possible solutions–by most representatives of theology as well as of the sciences–in reality, does not constitute a truly satisfying solution. It much rather resembles a state of mind–if transposed from the field of intellectual history to that of individual psychology–would have to be diagnosed as a classical case of schizophrenia. As a matter of fact, the experience of one and the same ultimate reality that we are faced with as human beings determines our religious as well as our scientific consciousness. Both modes of experiencing and interpreting this ultimate reality have been most intimately connected and interdependent throughout the ages.

1

Their not wanting to have anything to do with each other constitutes a completely exceptional state of affairs. It points to a profound split in our spiritual and mental attitude toward reality that is totally new in the intellectual history of the West. From the beginning of man's development of mind and spirit, religious and scientific consciousness has been in a state of dialectical tension, but this relationship had never been stabilized in the schizophrenic state of grim nonrecognition that seems to be the case today.

The topic of the present treatise is directly concerned with the interrelationship of the religious and the scientific consciousness. I attempt to demonstrate–using materials from theological and scientific sources that until now have been paid scant attention–how, during the course of the 18th century, the discovery of electricity and the simultaneous dicovery of magnetic and galvanic phenomena were accompanied by a most significant change in the image of God and in the concept of God's presence in the world, and as a consequence a completely new understanding of the relation of body and soul, of spirit and matter, of life and elemental substance.

The medieval concept of God and medieval Christology had for their central image that of light: God as the sun, as the light which radiates its powers into the world, including the soul and spirit of man. The conceptual and symbolic world of medieval belief in God consisted in a metaphysics of light that governed cosmology, epistemology and also scriptural exegesis.2

With the discovery of magnetism and electricity, a new image appeared beside the symbolism of light: Magnetism and electricity emerged as the most palpable manifestation of the hidden presence of divine power in the world and its objects–as the concealed power that creates life, movement and warmth; that permeates the entire universe; that causes the attraction of opposite poles that accumulates violent discharges from time to time and manifests itself in lightning as overpowering, blinding light, as destructive force in its numinous, irrational form. Electricity and magnetism became a new symbol for God.

For this also there had been several forerunners in medieval mysticism; the magnet had always been a symbol of God, a symbol of the enigmatic attraction of divine love that binds men filled with divine grace to Christ and to one another, a love that creates an intimate bond between believers and Christ without any external material ties, a love that fuses into *one* body the individual with the godhead, into an organism permeated by Christ's "magnetic" love for man and man's for Christ. Similarly, medieval emblematic mysticism contains many-sided usages of the magnet metaphor for the workings of the Holy

Ghost. In Book V of his "Cherubinischer Wandersmann," Angelus Silesius[3] sums up this idea in the following epigram (no. 130)[4]:

> The spiritual magnet and steel.
> God is a magnet, my heart is the steel.
> It always turns to Him as soon as He touches it.

NOTES

1. The most dependable contemporary study is Wolfgang Philipp's *Das Werden der Aufklärung in theologiegeschichtlicher Sicht* (Göttingen: 1957).

2. For the metaphysics of light, cf. Rudolf Bultmann, "Zur Geschichte der Lichtsymbolik im Altertum," *Philologus* 97 (1948): 1-36; Hans Meyer, *Geschichte der abendländischen Weltanschauung*, vol. 3 (Middle Ages) (Würzburg, 1948), p. 251 on Grosseteste and pp. 260ff. on Bonaventure; L. Baur, "Das Licht in der Naturphilosophie des Robert Grosseteste," *Beitrage zur Geschichte des Philosophie d. Mittelalter XVIII*, 4-6 (1917); Clemens Bäumker, "Witelo," *Beitrage III*, 2 (1908); E.R. Goodenough, *By Light Light* (New Haven, Conn., 1935); C. Kaliba, *Die Welt als Gleichnis des dreieinigen Gottes* (Stuttgart, 1952) ; A.C. Crombie, *Robert Grosseteste and the Origins of Experimental Science* (Oxford, 1953). See also the essays in *Studium Generale* 10 (1957): 432-447 (H. Blumenberg 13 (1960): 363-378 (J. Ratzinger) and 653-670 (J. Koch).

3. [Johann Scheffler (1624-1677) - ED.]

4. [In Schefflers *Sämmtliche Poetische Werke*, David A. Rosenthal (Regensburg, 1862). -ED.].

I

Rudolf Goclenius and Athanasius Kircher

It remained for the natural sciences and natural philosophy of the 17th and 18th centuries to investigate these relationships with a newly awakened scientific consciousness. This was more evident in the medical field than in any other.

In the 16th century Paracelsus (1493-1541) had initiated these investigations, studying the healing powers of the magnet and using it in therapy.[1] His initial probing was carried further in esoteric medicine and in the natural philosophy of Jakob Böhme and the Rosicrucians. Throughout the history of academic medical science, however, this therapeutic application of magnetism finds only occasional mention. The most important precursor of Mesmer was Rudolf Goclenius the Younger (his German name was Gockel) [1572-1621], Professor of Physics and Medicine at the University of Marburg since 1608. He was a cabalist of the first order, an astrologer and chiromancer well versed in all the occult arts.[2] In 1609, Goclenius wrote a book on the magnetic therapy for wounds,[3] in which he discussed the therapeutic application of the magnet in the form of a weapon salve–*unguentum armarium*–which, when applied to stab wounds and injuries due to blows, was supposed to heal them.

The Goclenius work is important in that it already contains a fully developed doctrine of magnetism according to natural philosophy. His point of departure lies in the precept that all of nature is imbued with an arcane force of attraction and repulsion that accounts for the innermost cohesion of the world. Innate in all things in the universe there is a quality of mutual alliance–*consortium*–and of separation–*dissidium*–with which, beyond any visible contact, they mutually influence and change one another, as experience proves. The exploration and recognition of these abstruse qualities and forces, so deeply concealed in nature's majesty, is natural magic (*magia naturalis*), which has its origin in the sympathy of things, and he who has recognized their harmony and their dissonance is called an authority on magic and–

5

using magic secretly–can bring forth admirable effects unbelievable to
the general public, so that one could believe they had only been produced with the help of demons, especially because the manner of their
production is totally unknown. This mystery, however, is nothing other than the science of sympathy and antipathy of higher and lower
things.[4]

    This doctrine regarding the cohesion in the universe between
"down" and "up"–between lower and higher spheres–condenses for Goclenius into an image of the universe as consisting of a single immense
living entity.

> All parts of this world of ours, however, depend upon the one
> creator and principle much as do the extremities of a living be-
> ing–*animal*–and they are tied to one another by means of the
> internal cohesion of the one and only nature: just as in us hu-
> man beings there exists mutual attraction and cooperation
> among brain, heart, lungs, liver, and other parts of the body,
> so that when one part suffers, all suffer. The extremities of this
> immense living entity behave in a like manner, i.e., all bodies
> of this world being joined together effect and suffer reciprocal
> influences and changes in their nature, and from this mutual re-
> lationship springs mutual love and from this mutual love re-
> ciprocal attraction (*communis attractio*). For this reason the
> magnet attracts iron, and the sun, flowers; this is why helio-
> tropic plants follow the movement of the sun while seleno-
> tropic ones follow that of the moon. This is why we on earth
> are able to observe the sun, the moon, and the other planets,
> according to the characteristics of earth. In heaven–to be sure,
> according to heaven's nature and modes of perception–one is
> able to observe stones, plants, and animals: so that in this
> manner one is able to recognize and search for the highest in
> the lowest sphere and the lowest in the higher one. God has de-
> creed in a law of fate that the lower sphere serve the higher.[5]

    The most comprehensive work on magnetism in the 18th cen-
tury was written by Athanasius Kircher (1602-1680), the most eminent Jesuit scholar in the sciences and the history of religion of the day,
who in 1643 published a voluminous work entitled *Magnes sive de
arte magnetica opus tripartitum*.[6]

    Athanasius Kircher's work has not yet been made the subject
of thorough investigation by scholars in the field of animal magnetism
as it was later developed by Franz Mesmer. Impeding such an investi-

gation has been the widespread conviction that there had been no influences on Mesmer's later medico-scientific thinking during his studies at the Dillingen Jesuit college, which served his preparation for the ministry and which he left to turn to medicine, a vocation better suited to his nature. It is probable, however, that during his studies at the Dillingen Jesuit college Mesmer was exposed to Kircher's ideas on magnetism.

As a matter of fact, all basic ideas of later so-called mesmerism are present in embryonic form in the work of Athanasius Kircher. His book *Magnes liber primus artis magneticae-De natura et facultatibus magnetis* is even to the modern reader an admirable compendium-overwhelming in the richness of its perspectives-of all of the insights concerning the phenomenon of magnetism that had been discovered and researched up to the time of its publication by the various divisions of the natural sciences.

Already the format of the book is interesting. Its frontispiece portrays the double-headed, electrified imperial eagle suspended on a magnetic chain from the imperial crown, which above the globe is supported by the cross. The cross itself bears a magnetized arrow pointing to the heavenly sun. Similarly, a magnetic arrow mounted in the crown points to the divine magnet. The imperial eagle itself is magnetized, carrying in its right claw three crowns, those of Hapsburg, Bohemia, and Hungary, and in its left claw the three scepters of these realms. The three crowns adhere to one another by means of magnetic force as do the three scepters. The magnetic power of imperial sovereignty radiates, in the form of arrows, onto the towns and castles of the country from in between the feathers of the spread wings. The arrows suggest the magnetic force of the empire's or Leopold III's authority. Leopold's portrait is shown on the eagle's breastplate and the work is dedicated to him. A Greek hymn to God, the universal magnet, ends the work. Beneath the hymn, a closing vignette shows the egg of Columbus, standing on its point on a slate, with the caption "*Et nos haec poteramus.*" ["That we could also have done!"] Here the author reveals himself as the scholar who–knowing the art of magic–is able to do the impossible and really balance the egg on its point. [See illustration p. 8]

The first book of the *Magnes sive de arte magnetica* treats of the nature and characteristics of magnetism; the second deals with its practical application in the various areas of technology. Of special significance is the third book, *Artis magneticae mundus sive catena magnetica*. This work depicts magnetism as an elemental force of nature, manifesting itself in a number of different yet interdependent phenomena in all nature's realms. The first part treats of the magnetism of the earth, of the planets and stars; the second, of the magnetic attributes of the elements; the third, of the magnetic force inherent in the entire earth and its heterogeneous parts–including the power of the divining rod and its use. The fourth part discusses the magnetism of the sun and the moon; the fifth, the magnetic force of plants. The sixth part deals with animal magnetism; the seventh, with magnetism in the field of medicine; the eighth, with the magnetism of music, and the ninth, with the magnetism of love.[7]

This external classification already attests to the fact that magnetism is here understood as *one*, if not *the* elemental force in nature that essentially holds the world together, and in whose sphere, according to Athanasius Kircher, belong not only physical phenomena but also those of the soul and the spirit. As Kircher states in his proem, he intends to prove in the third book that there exists an inner bond of unity *(nexum unionemque)* among all of the things becoming radiant in

our universe, and that their cooperation and mutual attraction can be explained only by a kind of magnetic power and quality.[8] He links his magnetic interpretation of the universe's essential cohesion to more ancient teachings about the mysterious fundamental force in nature, which was characterized by Plato's the "art of God" by Plato (*artem dei*), by the Greeks as the "unspeakable power" (*arrhetos dynamis*), as an "occult quality" by the Romans, as an "instrument of divine power" by the Hebrews, as a "concealed form that operates in all things" by the Arabs, and as the "sympathetic and antipathetic property" by other thinkers, and for which Athanasius here introduces the concept of magnetism. He is, to be sure, aware of the fact that he is breaking new ground by doing so.

> We are exploring the context of the entire universe and all of its corporeal objects in a new and singular fashion. Whosoever possesses the key to this method should know that he will find the door open to the knowledge of all concealed things; what is more, an open door to that true wisdom sought by the true philosophers, the wisdom called *magic*, and to the secrets of that true philosophy.[9]

In an impressive way, Athanasius Kircher illustrated the power of magnetism by means of a sunflower clock he himself constructed. Since ancient times the sunflower has been considered an illustration of the sun's power, since its blossoms constantly turn to the sun. In the third century B.C., Proclus regarded the sunflower as a symbol of the turning of individual reason in the human soul toward the indwelling divine reason. The sunflower emblem can be traced through the tradition of mystical allegorical images up to Angelus Silesius. In his "*Cherubinischer Wandersmann*,"[10] we find an epigram entitled "Solstice." It reads,

> Be not surprised, friend, that I won't look around,
> For I must always turn toward my sun.

In order to prove the magnetic basis of the sunflower's turning toward the sun, Athanasius Kircher invented a sunflower clock, of which a detailed drawing is reproduced as an etching in his work. In the center of a circular well floats a round pot in which a sunflower is planted. A metal circle is mounted, above the well's rim, at the height of the blossom. The 24 hours of the day and night are engraved on its inner surface. In the center of the sunflower's disk an arrow is stuck.

The placement of the sunflower in a freely moving container permits it to turn fully to the sun all day until the sun sets. Accordingly, the arrow accurately indicates the hours of the day on the hour circle. Athanasius Kircher proudly reports that this sunflower clock–the technical proof he crafted [to show] the effectiveness of magnetism in the plant kingdom–stood in his garden and functioned superbly while the sunflower was blooming.

    Athanasius Kircher's work on magnetism is of particular interest to historians of religion. It shows that, despite his formal adherence to a dogmatically correct concept of God, as he came under the influence of the idea of linking the image of the magnet and its associated phenomena with God, the personal elements in Athanasius Kircher's work and in his conception of God became less and less prominent. In their stead, the impersonal elements in his idea of God began to gain prominence, [as he came to see] God as an all-pervading power and radiance that gives life to, forms, and sustains everything. "God, the Magnet" [is referred to less often, and there are more and more allusions to] the magnetic force of nature.This depersonalization in the concept of God does not urge a theoretical, but rather a practical, equation of the divine spirit as *vis magnetica dei* with the all-animating power of nature. Already in Athanasius Kircher we frequently find a shift in perspective–a shift of which he himself was probably not aware–from the idea of the divine magnet to that of a magnetic, all-pervasive power, which essentially creates and guides not only order and life but also the preservation and continuation of the universe. There can be no doubt that it was especially this shift in emphasis that contributed to the development that became manifest in the pansophical theology of nature and that forms the transition to Mesmer's *evangelium naturae* [gospel of nature] and to the philosophy of nature in Romanticism.[11]

NOTES

1. See Paracelsus (Theophrastus Bombastus von Hohenheim), *Sämmtliche Werke*, ed. Karl Sudhoff and Wilhelm Matthiessen (Munich-Berlin, 1922-35), pt. 1: vol. I. p. 261; vol. II, pp. 49-57 ("On the Powers of the Magnet"), 123 ("On Natural Things"); vol. V, pp. 333, 335; vol. XIV, pp. 542, 650; pt. 2: vol. II, pp. 435ff. (I am indebted for these references to Dr. Kircher of the Marburg Paracelsus Institute.)

2. H. Hermelinck and S.A. Kahler, *Die Universität Marburg 1527-1927* (Marburg, 1927), p. 219.

3. *Tractatus de magnetica curatione vulnerum* (Marburg, 1609).

4. *Tractatus*, p. 15.

5. P. 18.

6. 2nd ed. (Coloniae Agrippinae, 1643). On Athanasius Kircher, see his autobiography, *Vita a semetipso conscripta,* ed. (with Kircher's letters) Ambros. Langenmantel (Augsburg, 1684); tr. into German by N. Seng (1901). There is a very one-sided treatment of Kircher by Ermann in ADB, vol. 16, pp. 1-4; a more reliable account is by K. Brischer, *P. Athan. Kircher, Ein Lebensbild* (Würzburg, 1877).

7. *Proömium* to bk. III, pp. 463ff. [On Kircher and the magnetism of music, see p. 16.–ED.]

8. *Proömium*, p. 464.

9. P. 463.

10. Bk. II, no. 251.

11. See the outstanding work by Hans Grasssl, *Aufbruch zur Romantik, Bayerns Beitrag zur deutschen Geistesgeschichte* (Munich, 1968), pp. 154ff. It includes material on Mesmer, his controversy with Gassner, and his victory at the Bavarian Academy.

II

Franz Anton Mesmer and
Benjamin Franklin

Subsequent developments took a divided course. The first
course was taken by Franz Mesmer [1734-1815];[1] [the other way was
followed by Franklin and the other early electricians]. Mesmer had become acquainted with the theology of magnetism while a student at
the Dillingen Jesuit Seminary and broadened these teachings on animal
magnetism to form the basis for a therapy, which gained very wide recognition throughout Europe. Characteristic differences are evident in
his teachings as compared with those of Kircher. First of all, he follows to its conclusion the process of depersonalizing the concept of
God that had its beginning in Kircher's work. Mesmer discards the entire terminology used in the dogmatic teachings of the Church and in
biblical theology and retains only the concept of magnetism as the secret, innermost life force of nature, his "gospel of nature" [*evangelium
naturae*]. Even though he maintained friendships with enlightened, ed-
ucated princes of the Church, priests, and theologians during his lifetime, he did not go to church, neither to confession nor to mass. There
is no cross on his headstone in Meersburg, but rather the divine eye in a
triangle, emitting rays, and the spiral of the planets. For him there existed no sacrament other than the "sacrament of nature."

But beyond this, his system of animal magnetism is not a doctrinaire construction, but rather a theoretical interpretation of his
charismatic talents as a physician and helper that had manifested themselves early on.

Compared with Athanasius Kircher, there is not much in Mesmer that is new in regard to theory. Strictly speaking, Mesmer was not
the kind of theorist who grasps phenomena by analyzing them intellec-
tually. Presenting his insights systematically by using theoretical concepts was not in his nature. Predominant in him were an intuitive feel-

ing for nature and the extraordinary charismatic talent of exerting a healing effect on his surroundings. What remained relevant to his thinking, ultimately, was the ever new and continuing experience of being in direct contact with the innermost force of nature and of being gifted with the ability to use this force for the benefit of those whose vital functions and relationships were disturbed. To him nature was no longer personalistic–in terms of the Christian belief in creation by a personal God–but rather present in the revelation of an inexhaustible power that gives life and form. The fact that he called this power "magnetism," which he himself sensed, was not fundamentally significant: he himself had vacillated for a long time wondering whether he should not call it "electricism." He decided on the term "magnetism" because it appeared to him that the power he sensed had a greater similarity to the characteristics of mineral magnetism. Kircher's description of magnetism as the all-encompassing universal vital force probably was the decisive factor–he also adopted Kircher's term "animal magnetism."[2]

For the very reason that Mesmer was experiencing a "force," it was difficult for him to conceptualize this experience; he himself felt that concepts fell far short of doing justice to the reality of the matter. Above all, Mesmer was totally unsuited to engage in discussions with representatives of academic medicine–he spoke a different language. Again and again he was astounded to find that his colleagues from the academy did not comprehend what to him was the self-evident basis for experiencing and intuiting life, and that they considered him a charlatan because he did not accept their theory of illness and healing methods. The conclusion of the Paris medical committee[3]– that there was no such thing as an animal magnetism and that, therefore, it could not effect any cure–appeared as absurd to him as it would have been to conclude that there was no sun in the sky and that, therefore, it could not radiate warmth to the earth. His only real defense consisted in lavishing his healing powers even more profusely, in healing even more patients, in penetrating his surroundings even more strongly with his magnetic influences, and in guiding the disturbed equilibrium of forces in the psychosomatic organism of the patient through crisis to harmony, i.e., to health. This was, to him, the only relevant proof of the accuracy of his theory.

In Mesmer, his person and his thought, his personal charisma and its emanations, and his teachings are inextricably bound together. Conversely, one may state that his printed teachings nowadays strike us as being strangely pale and that they only come to life when thinkers, such as, for example, Oken[4] or Wolfahrt[5]–who themselves possess a cosmic feeling for nature and a cosmic consciousness–interpret them and lend to them the life of their own intuitive experience. In this mystical atmosphere the old mystical tenet indeed holds true that states that only peers are able to recognize a peer.

This is most impressively confirmed by the autobiographical lines in which Mesmer himself describes his attempt to elevate to the conceptual sphere the experience of nature that is at the root of his magnetic praxis:

In 1775, for the first time, I informed the scholarly world of the existence of animal magnetism. . . .The system which guided me to the discovery of animal magnetism was not the fruit of a single day. The insights gathered by and by in my soul, just as the hours of my life accumulated. . . .

I was astonished by the coldness with which the first ideas I dared to make public were received. . .This poor reception induced me to examine my thoughts anew. . .

My entire soul was filled with a consuming fire. I no longer searched for truth out of a gentle inclination, I searched for it with extreme anxiety. I was only attracted by fields, forests and the remotest wilderness. They made me feel closer to nature. At times, in a state of most vehement emotions, I believed that my heart, exhausted from her futile luring, wildly rejected her. When overcome in this manner, I would shout, O nature, what is it you want of me? Soon, however, I would believe myself embracing her tenderly or entreating her, in a state of the highest impatience, to fulfill my wishes. Fortunately, my vehemence in the stillness of the woods was only witnessed by the trees. For, in truth, I must have looked like one insane. I began to hate all other activities. Any moment spent on them seemed like stealing from the truth . . .

I regretted spending time on finding words for my thoughts. And then I made a strange decision to free myself from this slavery. My imagination was so enormously tense that I endowed this abstract idea with the semblance of reality. For three months I thought without words.

When I concluded this thinking in depth, I looked around me in wonderment. My senses no longer fooled me as they had before. All objects appeared before me in a new form. The most common thought associations seemed to be in need of closer examination, and people appeared to be so exclusively tending toward being mistaken that I experienced a rapture never felt before as soon as I discovered a truth as clear as the sun veiled by commonly accepted opinions. . .

Unnoticeably peace entered my soul again, for it was now totally convinced of the actual existence of that truth I had heretofore pursued so feverishly. To be sure, I still saw it from a distance, still being veiled in a light mist, but I clearly perceived the path leading to it. . . . I still had ahead of me a long and difficult journey through the realm of other people's opinions. I saw the entire enormous road lying before me. But this did not discourage me. I much rather felt the need of increasing the number of obstacles by imposing upon myself the strictest duty of handing over to mankind the immeasurable treasure which God had entrusted to my hands—and to hand it over in its total purity, as unspoilt as I had received it from nature.

Animal magnetism, in my hands, has to be regarded as a sixth artificial sense. Senses can neither be explained nor described—they can only be felt, intuited. Trying to make the theory of color understandable to someone born blind would be in vain. One has to make him see, that is, make him feel. The same is true in regard to animal magnetism. Above everything else it wants to be felt, and only feeling it can make its theory understandable. . . .

I have dedicated my life to the happiness of mankind. . .

O truth! Truth! You will be victorious with undeniable certainty! But the beginning will be extremely toilsome, and the first steps will have to be taken daringly over innumerable thorns. . . The time will come when this truth will appear completely proved, and all of mankind will thank me for it.[6]

Although Mesmer presented his theory of animal magnetism only incompletely, in a form which satisfied neither academic medicine nor the academic philosophy of his age, Mesmer had the profoundest effect on theology as well as on the philosophy of religion in his time—effects that directly point to the beginnings of Christian Science and modern theosophy but also to the beginnings of modern psychoanalysis. These aftereffects, however, cannot be gone into here.

From a strictly scientific viewpoint, Mesmer contributed but little to the exploitation of the phenomenon of magnetism. The instruments he invented and used in the beginning of his medical practice—especially his so-called baquet—did not result from a physical exploration of magnetic phenomena. This baquet consisted of a bucket containing iron shavings and glass shards, which was filled with water and had iron bars stuck into it. This apparatus never generated any "magnetic currents"; it did, however, exert a strong psychic effect on those patients who touched the iron bars. Mesmer finally abandoned the use of the baquet completely after he realized that he could achieve therapeutic effects without the baquet, simply by holding up his index finger or looking at a patient. Furthermore, the baquet was only one element in a multitude of ways in which he influenced his patients' souls, including the near-darkness of his consulting room, which was equipped with velvet draperies, and the patients' touching one another as they formed a closed chain by holding hands. Mesmer's magician's robes and his equally "magical" playing of the tuned glasses[7] [also contributed to the effect].

The other course taken by Kircher's teachings on magnetism led to electricity's moving into the place that was held by magnetism. It could hardly be expected that Athanasius Kircher's contemporaries would be able accurately to distinguish electrical phenomena from those of magnetism. Mesmer had vacillated for a long time, wondering whether he should call the power that he observed and practiced animal magnetism or animal electricism. How could one discern differences [between the two modalities] when electricity could be engendered only by weak currents and was only available in low voltage? The only method of creating a current before the discovery of the Leyden jar had been the electric wand, with which a low voltage was engendered by means of rubbing it with a hairy cat fur or with discarded winter stockings, and this current was weak. The pioneers of electrical research had no knowledge of the vast force of atmospheric electricity, otherwise they would not have proceeded so carelessly. Only gradually, through contacts between such different explorers as Benjamin Franklin and Franz Mesmer, did there arise an awareness of the differences between magnetism and electricity. The encounter with Benjamin Franklin in Paris took a fateful meaning for Mesmer. Franklin had been the American ambassador to France since 1774, and at his house in Passy the luminaries of politics, the sciences, and commerce met. Soon after their meeting, Franklin was to turn away from Mesmer, an action reflecting the fact that the discovery of electricity had made immense progress and had reached such a degree of scientific sophistication and technical application that it freed itself from the confused identification with magnetism. It did so in the brutal manner of simply denying the existence of magnetism. Franklin had already passed through the period of his own development in the field of electricity, a period that encompassed the years from 1746 to 1752, and he was known in Europe as the most eminent expert on the newly discovered power called electricity.[8] No wonder then that he was looked upon as a magician, a view that found expression in his 1778 marble bust by Houdon, with its Latin epigram by Turgot:

Eripuit caelo fulmen sceptrumque tyrannis–
He wrested the flash of lightning from heaven and the scepter from the tyrants.

Here revolution merges with electricity.[9]

To be sure, Franklin did not consider himself the magician that his contemporaries claimed he was. A rationalist, he had already demythologized electricity and had robbed it of its numinous character through his lightning rod. Thus from the beginning he was skeptical toward Mesmer,who practiced his magnetic healing in a mystical half-light, behind draperies and to the accompaniment of mysterious music, and who himself wore the magician's long robes made from violet silk.

Despite this, there exist a number of noticeable convergences between Benjamin Franklin and Mesmer. Both of them were fascinated by newly discovered natural forces, one by the phenomenon of electricity, the other by the related phenomenon of magnetism. Both of them not only tried to understand forces but to control them for the benefit of mankind. Finally, while exploring this new natural force, both of them were led to the field of music and encountered–independent of each other–the same novel instrument, the glass harmonica.

The traces of this instrument's invention point to the great founder of magnetic theology and physics, Athanasius Kircher. In a chapter of his work on the magnet, he discussed magnetism in music.[10] Kircher interprets the vibrations caused by the tones of musical instruments as vibrations of a magnetic kind, and to demonstrate the connection that exists between magnetic currents and undulations in musical tones and in water, Kircher used glasses filled with water, which–when touched on the rims by a finger–emitted certain tones according to how full they were. Athanasius Kircher even calculated the mathematical connection between the pitch of a note and the height of the water level in the vibrating glass. His book also contains a drawing of five glasses filled with different fluids and standing next to each other on the same base. It also provides us with his reflections on the influence exerted by the kinds of fluids used on the pitch of notes and the tonal quality. [Illustration of Kircher's musical glasses, see p. 19.]

One should seriously consider the possibility that Mesmer–who was so strongly influenced by Kircher in his understanding of the

nature of magnetism and who had adopted the latter's concept of animal magnetism–also received from Kircher the suggestion for the
glass harmonica, the special instrument of "musical magnetism." Mesmer's own glass harmonica–used with great success in his magnetical
cures–is a direct development [from Kircher's device]. It was made of a
sounding-board on which there were placed, next to each other, a number of glasses that were tuned to a certain pitch on the musical scale,
and upon which one could play certain melodies as well as chords, the
latter through simultaneous rubbing of two glasses.

Franklin, too, was made aware of the glass harmonica through
the Royal Society in London, which described for him an instrument
claimed to have been invented by Richard Pockeridge[11] (Pockerich) in
1743. Franklin's description of the instrument, however, shows that
this instrument was a direct descendant of the one used in Athanasius
Kircher's experiments and designs. In a letter dated July 13, 1762, to
his friend Giambatista Beccaria in Turin, Franklin writes about Pockeridge:

> He collected a number of glasses of different sizes, fixed them
> near each other on a table and tuned them by putting into them
> water, more or less, as each note required. The tones were
> brought out by passing his fingers around their brims.[12]

That was exactly the kind of glass harmonica that Mesmer had been using in his early years in Vienna.

Franklin, however, was not satisfied with the construction of
this instrument. [Writing of an imitation of the Pockeridge instrument made by E. Deleval, he continues:]

> Being charmed with the sweetness of its tones, and the music
> he produced from it, I wished only to see the glasses disposed
> in a more convenient form, and brought together in a narrower
> compass, so as to admit of a greater number of tones, and all
> within reach of hand to a person sitting before the instrument.
> . . .[13]

Franklin considered it bothersome and impractical that the player had
to stand, bending over the table with its glasses, that so many glasses
were arranged next to one another and that they had to be filled with
fluid, which entailed the danger of breakage and spilling, but, above
all, that the pitch had to be corrected from time to time because evapo-
ration caused the water level to vary. Because of this, he totally dis-
pensed with fluids. Instead, he had poured 37 stemless glass bowls of
different diameter and thickness, bored holes in the center of their bas-
es and arranged them according to their individual tonal sequence on a
metal axis which–like early sewing machines–could be set in motion
by a flywheel connected by a transmission belt to a foot pedal. The
glasses themselves were ground or filed to attain their correct pitch.
All the glasses rotated on this axis simultaneously, the player sat
comfortably in front of the rotating axis and its glasses, and to play
the instrument it was only necessary to touch the individual rotating
glasses according to the sequence of desired notes on the musical scale
or to touch several glasses at the same time in order to produce the desired chord.[14] (See illustrations pp. 25, 26.)

He wrote in his letter to Beccaria:

London, July 13, 1752

Rev. Sir,

   I once promised myself the pleasure of seeing you at Turin,
but as that is not now likely to happen, being just about returning to my native country, America, I sit down to take leave
of you (among others of my European friends that I cannot see)
by writing.

   I thank you for the honourable mention you have so frequently made of me in your letters to Mr. Collinson and others, for

the generous defence you undertook and executed with so much
success, of my electrical opinions; and for the valuable present
you have made me of your new work, from which I have received great information and pleasure. I wish I could in return
entertain you with any thing new of mine on that subject; but I
have not lately pursued it. Nor do I know of anyone here that is
at present much engaged in it. . .
  In honour of your musical language, I have borrowed from it
the name of this instrument, calling it the Armonica.[15]

  Franklin's harmonica quickly became fashionable; business-
minded Franklin used his opportunity of having numerous copies of his
model produced in quantity in London,which were sold for forty guin-
eas apiece. The English artist Marianne Davies gave public concerts on
the Franklin model of the glass harmonica and demonstrated it on a
concert tour first in Italy and later at the Imperial Court in Vienna,
where Marie Antoinette became a student of hers. Thus, through his
harmonica, Franklin became a competitor of Mesmer in Vienna, and
Mesmer could read in the program of Marianne Davies the remarks
praising the use of the novel musical instrument, the invention of the
celebrated Doctor Franklin, as the concert's special attraction.[16]
  It goes without saying that the two instruments are strongly
different from each other in sound. While Mesmer's harmonica–in
which each glass had to be filled individually and rubbed individually–
produced a curiously magical tone, the tone of the rotating glass bowls
of Franklin had a much harder and more technical sound; it was harsher
and more penetrating. It is interesting to note that some Mozart com-
positions for glass harmonica were written for Mesmer, who had introduced Mozart to this instrument at his house.
  The tonal difference between the two glass harmonicas also
expressed the difference between the inventors. Mesmer was the magus of animal magnetism; the soft, mysterious, penetrating sound of
his glass harmonica which stimulated as well as calmed the nerves,
was part of the total magical style of his therapy. Franklin, on the other hand, no longer considered himself a magician but rather a practical
inventor and producer, a beneficiary of technology who was as interested in the efficiency of his inventions as he was in the income they
brought him. After he had succeeded in making harmless electricity's
flash of lightning–which until then had darted out of the clouds as a
sign of unpredictable, numinous divine power–by means of his lightning rod, the next step was to harness this force that nature so sense-
lessly wasted and to make it perform a useful and profitable service.

For this reason he had been interested, during his travels in England and on the Continent, in electrostatic machines and the medical application of electricity. He was profoundly impressed, when–while visiting the royal hospital in Hanover in 1766–he was shown a novel electrostatic machine that was used there for therapy and that administered especially strong electrical shocks.

When later on he met Mesmer in Paris, he approached him with curiosity and suspicion–suspicion, because he considered Mesmer's style eerie; curiosity, because he suspected magnetism to be a phenomenon related to, if not indeed identical with, electricity and because it was a force he did not know, which, however, he considered to be of practical use.

In the same spirit of watchfulness in which he had followed the development of French balloon experiments and experiments with phosphorous matches, he was interested in Mesmer's healing method, about which a great fuss was made in circles close to him, and to which Franklin's French friends such as Lafayette and Bergasse, both of them members of the Franco-American Society, were so enthusiastically devoted.[17]

His deep-rooted rationalism, however, from the first rendered him immune to a personal experience of magnetic phenomena. It is part of Mesmer's tragedy that the scientific qualities of Mesmer's animal magnetism were examined by people who by their mental attitude were totally immune to magnetic phenomena. [In the case of the] pure rationalist Claude Arien Helvétius–who one day appeared in Mesmer's treatment room in the Rue du Coq-Héron–neither the baquet nor Mesmer's magnetic strokes produced the slightest reaction; nor was the slightest magnetic reaction induced in La Harp–who came to Mesmer's place as a skeptical observer and underwent several experiments–by means of Mesmer's extended index finger, which in thousands of his more sensitive contemporaries had caused cramps, convulsions, screams of delight and terror, hypnotic sleep, and ecstasies. It was similar with Benjamin Franklin; he observed Mesmer with the cool and skeptical watchfulness with which nowadays a psychiatrist looks at the witchcraft performed by an Africanmedicine-man.

Because of Franklin's reputation as an expert on electrical questions in the learned circles of Paris, and since he was interested in as well as critical of Mesmer, one can easily understand his appointment as an expert to the committee of scientists that was formed at the King's order on March 12, 1784, which was charged with exploring the scientific basis of animal magnetism and the treatment and cures issuing from it. At first the committee consisted of only four physicians nominated by the medical school. These four asked to have their number enlarged by members of the Académie des Sciences, which then chose five members: Franklin and his friends Alphonse LeRoy, Jean Bailly, and Antoine Lavoisier, and the mathematician M. de Borie.[18]

Franklin himself, however, did not regularly participate in the examinations held by the committee in tiresome individual meetings, since he fell ill during this time and found the trips to Paris to attend the meetings too wearying. For the sake of his comfort, he succeeded in having a change made so that the examinations of the magnetic treatment methods took place at his own house in Passy. Thus physicians and patients of mesmerism moved to his home: Franklin took part in several séances at his house and subjected himself also to magnetic manipulations–but, as in the case of Helvétius, without success. Soon after the committee had been established, he made skeptical remarks about Mesmer's theory of animal magnetism and credited all cures to the imagination, not to the actual existence of a force like animal magnetism.

In spite of this, Franklin did not reject mesmerism as a healing method, but rather granted it a certain importance–at least for a certain segment of the population–especially under the aspect of psychogenetic healing.

[Franklin noted that]

> the delusion may . . . in some cases be of use while it lasts. There are in every great rich city a number of persons who are never in health because they are fond of medicines and always taking them, whereby they damage the natural functions and hurt their constitutions. If these people can be persuaded to forbear their drugs in expectation of being cured by only the physician's finger or an iron rod pointing at them, they may possibly find good effects though they mistake the cause.[19]

Thus Franklin envisioned a positive social function for the physician in the role of magician a la Mesmer, one based not on his "magic," but rather on the effect of human imagination, which can indeed lead to a cure in cases of psychogenetic illnesses.

NOTES

1. On Mesmer, see the following works: Rudolf Tischner and Karl Bittel, *Mesmer und sein Problem, Magnetismus-Suggestion, Hypnose* (Stuttgart, 1941); F. Schurer-Waldheim Sen., *Anton Mesmer, ein Naturforscher ersten Ranges, Sein Leben und Werken* (Vienna, 1930); Bernhard Milt, "Franz Anton Mesmer und seine Beziehungen zur Schweizerische Magie und Heilkunde zu Lavaters Zeit," *Mitteilungen der antiquarischen Gesellschaft (Zürich)* 38, 1 [year unknown]. In Werner Leibbrand, *Romantische Medizin* (Hamburg-Leipzig, 1937), see especially chap. 5, "Tierischer Magnetismus und romantische Totalität," pp. 119-143; in Liebbrand, *Die speculative Medizin der Romantik* (Hamburg, 1956), see pp. 174-200 on animal magnetism. See also Stefan Zweig, *Die Heilung durch den Geist* (1931), which includes sections on Mesmer, Mary Baker Eddy, and Freud.

2. Pt. VI of bk. I discusses *De magnetismo animalium* (in the *De arte magnetica*). See n. 10.

3. [See infra, p. 37.]

4. Oken was the editor of *Isis*, the leading German scientific journal and founder of the annual conventions of German scientists and physicians. On Oken's relationship with Mesmer, see Milt, "Franz Anton Mesmer," pp. 117ff.

5. On Wolfahrt's relationship with Mesmer, see Milt, pp. 119ff.

6. Cf. Tischner and Bittel, *Mesmer und sein Problem*, p. 61.

7. [Although Benz uses the term "glass harmonica" to cover both Mesmer's and Franklin's instruments, Mesmer's was probably identical with Kircher's tuned glasses. It was Franklin who gave it the name "armonica." Some of his contemporaries began to add the "h" before the word, and it became generally known as the "glass harmonica." The harmonica or mouth organ was not invented until 1829 by the London firm of Wheatstone. –ED.]

8. Cf. Carl Van Doren, *Benjamin Franklin* (New York, 1938), pp. 384ff.

9. Cf. Helmut Hirsch, "Mesmerism and Revolutionary America," *American-German Review* X (October 1943), pp. 11-14 on the political implications of mesmerism.

10. Kircher, *De arte magnetica*, bk. III: *Sive catena magnetica*, Pt. VIII: *De magnetismo musicae*, on the glass harmonica (with an illustration), p. 751.

11. *Dictionary of National Biography*, vol. 45, p 451, s.v. "Pockeridge."

12. Benjamin Franklin to Beccaria, Torino [Turin], July 13, 1762. In *The Papers of Benjamin Franklin*, ed. L. W. Labaree (New Haven, 1966), vol. 10, p. 127.

13. Ibid.

14. *Papers*, p. 130.

15. Ibid.

16. Van Doren, *Benjamin Franklin*, p. 347.

17. See Louis Gottschalk, *Lafayette between the American and the French Revolution (1783-1789)* (Chicago, 1950).

18. [The commissioners' report also credits the sensations produced in mesmerism to "imagination."] See: *Report of Dr. Benjamin Franklin and Other Commissioners, Charged by the King of France with the Examination of the Animal Magnetism, as now Practiced at Paris; translated from the French . . (London, 1785).

19. Van Doren, p. 714.

FRANKLIN GLASS HARMONICA
Photograph of the actual glass harmonica made by Franklin
(c. 1765) for his putative mistress in Paris, Madame Brion.
(From the collections of the Bakken Library)

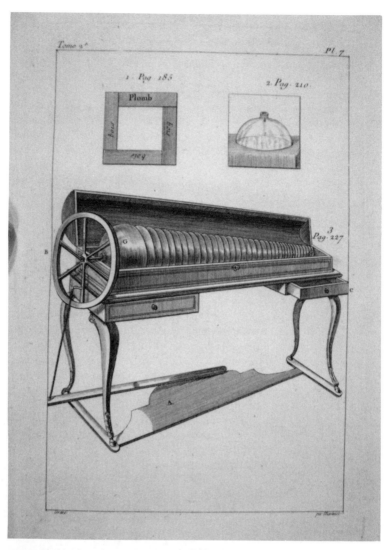

FRANKLIN GLASS HARMONICA
From *Œuvres de M. Franklin, Docteur ès Loix. . .*, translated
into French from the 4th English edition, vol. 2 (Paris, 1773).
(From the collections of the Bakken Library)

III

The Electrical Theologians–
Oetinger, Fricker, and Divisch

The masters proper of electrical theology are three personages, Friedrich Christoph Oetinger, Johann Ludwig Fricker, and Prokop Divisch. Only one of them has so far been given the attention of church historians: Friedrich Christoph Oetinger. He is the famous founder of the theosophical movement in Württembergian Pietism. He occupies an eminent position in the history of the sciences and theology of the 18th century, since he combined–in an entirely singular fashion for his time–a universal theological education with a surprisingly varied knowledge of the most important fields of scientific scholarship of the age. Thus all of his works reflect an intensive critical concern with Newton's new astronomy, with the mathematical and physical findings of Leibniz, with the medical teachings and methods of such great medical men as Leeuwenhoek and Boerhaave, as well as with the latest developments in geology, botany, and zoology.

While there is at least occasional mention by church historians of his work in the sciences named, Oetinger's part in the exploration of electricity, the newest field of scientific research of that time, has remained totally hidden from scholars, and especially the fact that he developed a complete electrical theology from his insights into electricity. Only the discovery of his correspondence with the other great *theologus electricus* of his day–the Premonstratensian Prokop Divisch [1696-1765] from Moravia–has made it possible to demonstrate this hitherto unknown aspect of his work in natural philosophy and theology and to clarify numerous statements and contexts regarding his scientific and theosophical discoveries that had not been observed or understood before.

The personal relationship between Oetinger and Divisch is of the greatest interest to the history of science; we can only marvel at the fact that it has not been mentioned in any previous work on Oeting-

27

er. The Swabian Protestant dean's relations with the Moravian Roman
Catholic priest and Premonstratensian monk were established through
Johann Ludwig Fricker, the most gifted among Oetinger's students.
Several biographical remarks in Oetinger's writings allow us to trace
the course of events.

Johann Ludwig Fricker[1] (1729-1766) was the son of a Stuttgart surgeon and studied theology and natural sciences in Tübingen.
Even though rooming in the city, he participated in the pietistic meetings at the Tübinger Stift, the boarding school for students of theology. While in Tübingen, he frequently visited Oetinger in Walddorf and
was permitted to participate in his chemical studies. In his autobiography Oetinger himself gives an account of how he intervened in Fricker's fate:

> Before I take leave of Walddorf, I have to relate the following.
> I had much edification in my parish, and many students came to
> me from Tübingen. Count von Castell also came to see me and
> asked that I put him in touch with a student strong in mathe-
> matics and well-versed in astronomy. I asked an M.A. by the
> name of Fricker to come over from Tübingen. He met with the
> count's approval, who took him along to see the artist Ness-
> tfell at Wiesentheid in Franconia in order to assist the latter in
> completing his celestial machine.Nesst fell was a joiner who
> day and night studied the heavens by means of binoculars and
> telescopes. Without a teacher he became knowledgeable in ce-
> lestial motion. This came to the attention of the Roman Em-
> peror.[2] The latter summoned him and Nesstfell promised to
> build a machine, which can still be seen in Vienna and
> Würzburg. Fricker was better at arithmetic than was Nesstfell.
> He had to rebuild half of the machine and construct it according
> to Bengel's future calculation. That was done. Then Fricker had
> to travel to Vienna where he waited for the Emperor's sum-
> mons; but he grew impatient. After his departure the Emperor
> wanted to summon him and was angry to learn that Fricker had
> been allowed to leave. He would surely have employed him.[3]

Oetinger once again reports on these important beginnings of
Fricker's scholarly development in the second part of his work on the
terrestrial and celestial philosophy of Swedenborg:

> J. L. Fricker, a learned pastor at Dettingen unter Urach, studied
> in Tübingen, perfected himself in mathematics from early on,

helped to perfect Nesstfell's astronomical machine located in Vienna. Spent some time at the Berlin intermediate school; later on stayed several months with the famous *electricus* Divisch in Moravia; traveled to the Cremniz mines in Hungary, and as a natural scientist everywhere searched for what is most real in physics. Found a totally new foundation for the musical scale, about which he conferred with me a great deal when I was the pastor at Walddorf in order to raise this theory to the level of psychological considerations.[4]

Fricker, therefore, paid his visit to Divisch from Vienna, where Fricker had traveled in the company of Nesstfell, the inventor of the astronomical clock. The clock itself was a technical representation of Swabian eschatology. It was constructed in such a way as to show the entire future course of the solar system until the time of Christ's second coming, the event that was to bring the course of the world clock to an end–according to Bengel's calculations at Easter 1834. As was the case with other technical wonders of the age–e.g., the lightning rod of Prokop Divisch–this technical invention was intended to be demonstrated to the Emperor. Through an arrangement with Count Lutz von Castell, a cousin of Count Zinzendorf, Fricker became the assistant to the joiner Nesstfell, the inventor of the world clock, so that he could help him perfect the clock and demonstrate it to the Emperor.

Fricker made use of his time in Vienna by acquainting himself with the most recent scientific developments in the intellectual life of the city. Thus he could report to his teacher and sponsor Oetinger on the magnetic cures of the Viennese Jesuit father Hell and the no less sensational cures of the latter's disciple and competitor Franz Mesmer from Itznang on Lake Constance. Most importantly, however, he instigated personal correspondence between Oetinger and Prokop Divisch while in Prendiz, and thus he inaugurated an intellectual friendship that was to bear the most meaningful fruit.

During Fricker's sojourn at the Prendiz parsonage, Divisch exerted a lasting influence on his guest through his blend of scholarly research and deep Christian piety, so that the Fricker's Protestant beliefs, in which he had been raised, were exposed to severe temptation. These were times when Protestantism was officially persecuted in the Hapsburg Empire through the application of the religious laws of the counter-reformation; in Württemberg the struggle was still raging between the denominations, between the Catholic Oberland and the Protestant Unterland. But the Swabian Protestant theologian Fricker–

who had brought his anti-Catholic resentment, in which he had been raised, from Tübingen to Vienna–came to know a Catholic cleric whom he was to love and admire as a scholar as well as a pious Christian. Karl Friedrich Hartmann, the well-known lyricist, reports in his diaries how it took a hard inner struggle for Fricker to overcome this confusion into which his encounter with Divisch's personality had plunged him:

> When Fricker was visiting Divisch in Moravia and came to realize that there was truth in this man also, he grew very thoughtful. And as he was still restless at that time, and as his philosophy caused him unrest, he decided to convert to Catholicism, as long as there was truth with Catholics also. In his restlessness and worry he prayed to God for certainty; while praying he felt as though he could see his own heart from which a bright, gentle, and blue flame was breaking forth, whereupon calmness and peace entered his heart.[5]

After his return, Fricker was employed as master of the household and tutor by Oberkriegskommissar Johann Christoph Oetinger, a brother of the theologian Oetinger. A year and a half later he gave up this position and accepted an appointment as tutor at the house of the rich merchant van der Vliet in Amsterdam, who belonged to a group of pietistic Mennonites. When accompanying van der Vliet on a trip to England, he met John Wesley[6] and George Whitefield.[7] After further travel and change of employment, he returned to Franconia in 1760. He stayed at the castle of Count Lutz von Castell, Oetinger's friend. At the same time he was helping Nesstfell complete a new astronomical world machine that was being built for the Prince-Bishop of Würzburg. Without doubt, Fricker was the author of the essay published under Nesstfell's name, *Beschreibung der Kopernikanischen Planetenmachine nebst Erklärung des vielfältigen Gebrauchs . . .* [8] After returning home in early 1761, he held several church positions in Kirchheim, Uhingen, and Dettingen, where he died on September 13, 1766. Throughout his life he was attached to Oetinger in loyal friendship and affection.

During his lifetime Fricker published none of his writings except for those essays that Oetinger included in his books. His most important work, *Unvollständige, je doch brauchbare Überbleibsel,"*[9] was posthumously published in 1775. Oetinger himself greatly appreciated and admired his student, who, he felt surpassed him by far, especially in mathematics and natural science.

The scholarly relationship that Fricker arranged between Divisch and Oetinger soon developed into a deep and truly congenial friendship in which both contributed and received equally. Oetinger, who was overwhelmed by Divisch's insights into the secrets of electricity, without envy acknowledged his superiority in this new field of natural science and recognized him as the true "magician from the Orient" who possessed the yearning for [Knowledge of the innermost secrets. Lit. "*zentraler kentnis.*" –ED.] lost for centuries–and had command over the miraculous gift's practical application. On the other hand, Oetinger spared no effort to help gain public recognition in Germany for Divisch, whose scientific findings were progressively misunderstood in his home country.

Prokop Divisch[10] was born at Senftenberg in Moravia on August 1, 1696. He first joined the Premonstratensian Order. This order was open-minded toward modern natural science; Divisch was given the opportunity to pursue his scientific interests in his capacity of teacher at the order's school. But since his duties as a member of the order made too great a demand on his time, he asked to be given a small parish that would allow him to devote more time to his scientific studies. Thus he was made the parson of Prendiz near Znaim in 1740, a village in which he quietly studied meteorology and wrote his *magnum opus* on meteorological electricity. It was here also that he utilized his findings and invented the first lightning rod–chronologically before Franklin, but blessed with less success.

For a time, to be sure, the Emperor's favor seemed to be beckoning. In 1750 he was asked to demonstrate his electrical inventions to Emperor Franz Josef and Empress Maria Theresa. His practical demonstration--he showed how electricity was discharged from the numerous points of the apparatus he had invented--was met with the most gracious acclaim and led to the awarding of several gold medals as indication of the Emperor's esteem.

Following the tragic death of a scholar who was killed while studying atmospheric electricity, Divisch was hoping for a measure of recognition for his research in Europe. Georg Wilhelm Richman[11] [1711-1753] had become a member of the Petersburg Academy of Sciences in 1741. In his studies of physics he devoted his time especially to the observation of electrical phenomena during thunderstorms, and for this purpose he invented an electrometer that was connected by means of a metallic conductor to an iron rod that protruded above the roof of his house. When on July 26, 1763, he heard distant thunder, Richmann hurried to his apparatus to measure the atmospheric electricity. When he bent over the terminal of the metallic conductor leading from the roof to his room, a whitish-blue ball of fire jumped the distance of one foot from the wire to Richmann's head and he fell to the ground, dead. With him in the same room was the Petersburg Academy's engraver, Sokolov, who had been commissioned to make engravings of the instruments for publication by the Academy. He was knocked to the ground unconscious but survived.

There is a report on Richmann's death written by M. W. Lomonossov that is of great interest because Lomonossov[12]-himself a physicist and a member of the Petersburg Academy of Sciences–lived in the same house as Richmann and was using the electrometer for measuring electricity in the same wire through which Richmann was struck dead. This happened at the time of the accident, in another room only a few meters away from Richmann. Lomonossov's remarks are perhaps also of interest, since Lomonossov had received most of his academic training at the University of Marburg as a student of Christian Wolff, whom he praises as *vir illustris supra mortalium sortem positus* and who had gone to great pains for the sake of his Russian student's scientific advancement. Lomonossov established a permanent link to Marburg by marrying a Marburg woman, Elisabeth Christine Zilch, "the late citizen Heinrich Zilch's legitimate daughter whom he left here in the care of the city aldermen and church presbyters." Even though Lomonossov belonged to the orthodox faith, they were married in the Marburg Reformed Protestant church, now the University chapel, on June 6, 1740.[13] His wife also plays a role in his letter to Minister Schuwalow, who was in charge of the Academy's affairs. This letter was written but a few hours after Richmann's death and reads:

> I consider it a miracle that I am writing your Grace now, because the dead cannot write. I do not know yet or am at least doubtful whether I am alive or dead. What I am saying is that Professor Richmann has been killed by lightning under the very same circumstances in which I found myself at the time. At one o'clock in the afternoon of July 26, a thundercloud rose from the North. The thunder was extraordinarily strong, but there was not a drop of rain. I was looking at the thunder machine we had set up [the electrometer constructed by Lomonossow and Richmann for measuring atmospheric electricity] but could not detect the slightest sign of electrical force. When dinner was being served, I expected strong electrical sparks from the wire, and for this reason my wife and the others stepped up and, just as myself, frequently touched the wire and the iron switch suspended from it, because I had wanted reliable

witnesses for the color of the [electrical] fire, concerning which the late Professor Richmann and I had just been arguing. Suddenly there was a terrible thunder clap just when my hand was touching the iron, and sparks were crackling. They all ran away from me, and my wife asked me to move away also. But curiosity kept me there for another two or three minutes until I was told that the soup was getting cold and until the electrical force had almost vanished.

I had been at table for only a few minutes, when the late Professor Richmann's servant suddenly opened the door, panting with tears and horror. He could hardly utter the words, "*profèssora gròmom saschiblò*" [a vernacularism, roughly translatable, "The professor has been rubbed out by lightning"]. In utter terror, my strength almost failing me, I ran to him and saw Richmann lying on the ground, dead. His poor widow and his mother, too, were as pale as he. The realization that death had just passed me by, his pale body, the understanding and friendship that had united us, the wailing of his wife and children: all of this assaulted my feelings to an extent that made it impossible for me to answer any of the questions directed to me by a multitude of people who had come running. I could only look at the face of the person with whom I had been conferring just an hour ago, discussing the planned public meeting. The first shock had jumped from the wire, suspended by means of a string, to his head, leaving a cherry-red mark on his forehead. Then the electricity had jumped into the floor boards from his feet. His foot and toes were blue, his shoe torn but not burned. We attempted to get his circulation going again, because he was still warm, but his head was injured and there was no hope. Thus through his lamentable experience he has furnished evidence proving that the electrical force of lightning can be diverted, however, to an iron rod that has to stand in an empty space which lightning can strike as ofen as it desires.

Lomonossov continues:

Otherwise Herr Richmann died a beautiful death in fulfillment of his professional duties. He will never be forgotten. In any case, I am of the opinion that this accident should not be used to impede the advancement of science, and I humbly ask you to continue furthering the sciences.[14]

There was a very excited discussion about the death of this researcher in Europe's learned circles. Divisch felt that his hour had come. At that time, in Prendiz, they already knew the maxim that nowadays is disseminated throughout the world: Touching of electrical wiring prohibited! Danger! Professor Euler, the most famous mathematician of the time and a Petersburg Academy colleague of Richmann, was sent a treatise by Divisch in which the danger was pointed out in the method used by Richmann and in which Divisch propagated his own method of "diverting the dangerous fire from the clouds without exposing oneself." In his work on the theory of meteorological electricity, Divisch comments on Richmann's death:

> Several weather experiments have recently come to our attention. I was informed about them by Vienna and Prague, and I was asked my opinion. In my answer to Baron von Gemmingen, the most honorable commanding officer of the highly respected Kasencian Regiment, I stated–and demonstrated in an electrical experiment--that the experiment with said rod was not only useless but also dangerous. This was shortly thereafter confirmed by sad results, since several people–among them the famous Professor Richmann of Petersburg–have been killed by lightning during such experiments. I also wrote a report on this unhappy experiment and sent the same to Berlin in 1754 so that it could be presented by Herr Euler, in his capacity as director of the Academy and famous professor there, and could be evaluated in consultation with others; however, I have received no reply to it.
>
> In spite of the fact that I did not receive a response, I decided to construct this weather machine–which was accomplished with God's help in 1755, by which (be it said to the glory of God) all harm [due to lightning] has been averted and which has been found to be flawless up to the present time, as has been made known to the world in the public newspapers, an article on which I have enclosed herewith; and through its use I have established my electrical theories and have intended to convey the same in sincere devotion to the learned world.[15]

A decisive success evaded Divisch, however, both at home and abroad. When in 1755 he proposed to the Emperor that he install lightning rods at the Hofburg, the imperial residence in Vienna, for the sake of His Majesty's safety, and when in this regard the monarch asked the mathematicians of the Vienna Academy for an opinion, they responded in the negative, even frightening the Emperor by claiming that the lightning rods might even guide electricity to the imperial residence and change it into a dangerous abode licked about by lightning--thus rendering a definitive judgment against Divisch's invention. Abbot Marci had to console Divisch with the remark, "Those who blaspheme are ignorant." Not until 1775, a decade after Divisch's death, was the first lightning rod installed in Hapsburg's domain, at the Count Nostiz castle at Mieschitz, and second, in 1776 on the Wyshegrad in Prague.[16]

Not only at the imperial court but also in Divisch's Prendiz parish, the invention of the lightning rod by the *theologus electricus* was not met with understanding. After the collapse of his proud plan of crowning the Vienna Hofburg with his invention, Divisch erected a lightning rod atop his own parish house, but the Moravian peasants regarded the new installation with the greatest suspicion and thought it the work of the devil. When a great drought spread in 1775, it was generally ascribed to the lightning rod of parson Divisch, which, it was thought, guided all electricity from the air to the ground, thus preventing precipitation, and one night the ministerial lightning rod was totally destroyed by perpetrators unknown.

Benjamin Franklin also had played unsuspectingly with the dangerous fire from the clouds, without premonitions, as had Richmann, but with better luck. With the assistance of his son, Franklin launched his first experimental kite in a harvested Maryland tobacco field in June of 1752 in the face of a brewing thunderstorm, and when the strings dangling from the kite assumed a horizontal position, thus indicating that the kite was charged with electricity, Franklin coolly touched the rain-soaked string to which the kite was fastened with his finger and received a tremendous electric shock–"a very evident electric spark."[17] Having survived the shock thanks to his robust nature, he himself invented the lightning rod. Franklin has gone down in the history of science as its inventor, in connection with which his successful participation in the American Revolution further strengthened his fame as a scientist. But Divisch disappeared in the shadow of Benjamin Franklin, who attracted the attention of all of Europe as the ambassador of the United States during his Paris sojourn. Only Soviet science reinstated the honor of the Moravian natural scientist who had been unjustly forgotten, by dedicating as an essay to him in the *Bolschaja Sovjetskaja Enciklopedia*; but there, on the Procrustean bed of dialectical materialism, he is also short-changed in a doctrinaire manner: he is given credit, to be sure, for his scientific accomplishments, but no mention is made of the fact that he was a Premonstratensian monk, the parson of Prendiz and a *theologus electricus.*[18]

Divisch was also unlucky in the publication of his scientific research. He had, to be sure, the respect of the people around him for his attempt to manipulate lightning and render it harmless through a technical contraption. A distich in his honor reads:

> Non laudate Jovem, gentes! Quid vester Apollo?
> Iste magis Deus est fulminis atque soni!
> [Why don't you heathens stop praising Jupiter and
>   Apollo!
> This one here is the greater god of sound and lightning!]

In spite of this, the works of "the greater god" were not being printed in Catholic Austria. Some sentences in his electrical theology were even censured for being offensive–with reference made to the canons of the Lyon Council–by a Church censor appointed by his clerical superiors in Vienna.[19]

After the invention of the lightning rod had slowly succeeded, it became the object of vehement theological discussion among the pious. Was not the erection of ligtning rods on public and private buildings, on churches even, an intrusion into the enforcement of divine justice and, therefore, a sin in the truest sense of *superbia*, the insolent human defiance of God? Was not the erection of a lightning rod ultimately an expression of a sacrilegious attitude toward God, which could be summed up roughly in the formula, "Surprise, surprise! You can't hit me!" For centuries clergymen of all denominations had used the occasion of fires caused by lightning in church steeples to make fires the subject of rousing penitential sermons that interpreted the divine flash of lightning as a special warning from God to remedy established communal abuses and as a direct divine call for spiritual and ethical renewal. Now, however, the direct enforcement of justice via lightning from the clouds was restricted, by means of man's technical intervention, to innocent schoolchildren on their way to school, to innocent shepherds in the fields, and to lovers under a tree who had missed hearing the brewing of a thunderstorm.

The problem of the lightning rod's permissibility was much discussed in contemporary sermons and in the press of that time. The answer to the problem was given totally in the spirit of a Rationalism that was already triumphant: the erection of lightning rods for man's protection was likened to the therapeutic endeavors of medicine, which for a long time nobody had regarded as an intrusion into divine jurisdiction. Thus it is stated in the "Preliminary Look Backward" [lit. *vor-*

erinnerung] to the German edition of a work by Benjamin Franklin:

> Since-so they say--the most highly regarded gentleman's bene-
> ficial invention that protects buildings from lightning has no
> longer been looked upon as an intervention in the omnipo-
> tence of God; since that time even relatively timid people have
> been persuaded to look upon the extension of Franklin's teach-
> ings to the securing of entire regions, cities, townships and
> fields against climatic devastation as a legitimate means of
> averting great disasters which, strictly speaking, are a punish-
> ment, and they do so while praying for God's mercy; in the
> same way men attempt to avert other great evils, such as the
> plague, from mankind without daring to intervene in God's om-
> nipotence, from the basic and natural instinct of self-
> preservation.[20]

The pastor of Prendiz was in a difficult position considering
the numerous scientific and theological attacks on him. In this situation, the Protestant Dean of Denkendorf in faraway Württemberg
proved to be his only reliable friend; he went to great lengths in an attempt to help "the Magician from the Orient" in practical ways, in
translating the distant friend's work of a lifetime into German and in
having it published in Tübingen. Divisch's work, *Theorie von der meteorologischen Electricité* [21] a whole compendium of treatises, the first
document in German scientific literature on the subject of electricity.
Once more it conjures up the time around 1755 when Divisch performed his electrical experiments at the Imperial Court. According to
Divisch's wishes–who died during the year of publication in Prendiz–
the work is dedicated to Emperor Francis I who, as it were, passed
away in the year of the German book edition and was no longer in need
of a lightning rod. In his dedicatory epistle to the deceased the inventor
states:

> The most gracious sentiments Your Imperial Majesty were so-
> kind as as to lavish on several samples of my electrical re-
> search and pursuits–sentiments I most deeply appreciate--even
> then prompted me to publish a most humble token of the feel-
> ings that were aroused in me due to Your most gracious recep-
> tion of my negligible endeavours. As I am attempting to ac-
> complish my intentions by means of publishing this booklet,
> I am hopeful that Your majesty's praiseworthy tendencies in fa-
> vor of scholarship will let You be pleased with this evidence of
> my deepest veneration.

To Oetinger personally the correspondence with Divisch was of vital importance, so important that he makes mention of it even in his biblical dictionary. In its article on "Fire"–as in so many of its other articles–he refers to his beloved [friend] and highly esteemed *theologus electricus* Prokop Divisch, "a man with whom I corresponded to the day of his death."[22]

In the introduction to his translation of Divisch's lifework, Oetinger reports in even greater detail on the author and reveals the fact that Fricker–who had first established contact between the two theological electricians–had also collaborated in the translation of Divisch. Oetinger writes,

> People would have welcomed long ago the public dissemination of the theory of electricity by Divisch who for a long time has gained fame in newspapers. Finally the opportunity is offering itself. . . . The following persons have assisted me in [translating this work]: the highly learned and highly esteemed Pastor Fricker who through lengthy familiarity with Herr Divisch learned to gain the best insight into his meaning; and, further, several intelligent scholars, especially Herr Magister Rösler, the Very Reverend Herr Consistory-Councillor's son–in this repect distinguished by superb learning–who himself has gained fame due to his theological-physical work *De Luce Primigenia* and who has gathered together all electrical discoveries. I, therefore, surrender the work to all those who take pleasure in establishing links between theology and physics.[23]

This clearly shows that Oetinger had meanwhile expanded his circle of electrical specialists. M. Rösler (1740-1790) who is mentioned here, was the son of Gottlieb Friedrich Rösler who after his tenure as coach at the Tübingen Seminary was a professor in the "Oberes Gymnasium" in Stuttgart (1734-1752) and Consistory-Councillor and Abbot of Alpirsbach from 1752 to 1766. His son also was named Gottlieb Friedrich. Born in Stuttgart on July 24, 1740, he studied theology at Tübingen, received his "magister" degree in 1759 and served as Deacon in Lauffen on Neckar from 1766 to 1767. Due to his scholarly merits in the field of natural sciences, he was appointed Professor of Mathematics and Physics at the Stuttgart "Ober gymnasium" in which he taught until 1783 and where he died in 1790. Rösler was preoccupied with problems of electricity. His most important publication is an electrical interpretation of light on the first day of

Creation, the *De Luce Primigenia*, published in 1764.[24] Thus the work precedes the publication of Prokop Divisch's *Theorie*, in whose German translation from the Latin manuscript Rösler participated, according to Oetinger's report, but it presupposes knowledge of the chronologically later publication. In his dissertation Rösler speaks of Prokop Divisch of Moravia as "the untiring examiner of nature" and points to the "principles of this man's system which have hitherto been quite unknown." In the respective footnote he announces the impending edition of these fundamental principles when he states,

> It offers hope that the principles which [Divisch] discovered some time ago in experiments and which he reduced to a system—and which he will call *Meteorologiam et Magiam* ("Meteorology and Magic")—may very soon be in the public domain.[25] It commends itself not only by its novelty but also by the profundity of Herr Divisch, a man who is worthy indeed to experience favor linked with Imperial grace—a favor in which he takes no common pleasure—as well as the acclaim of those *outside the realm*.[26]

There can scarcely be any doubt that the thesis of Rösler's own dissertation was influenced by Divisch's work which, as it were, has as its point of departure the characteristic interpretation of the light on the first day of Creation as the "electrical fire" that from the first day on was added to matter and was referred to as "Nature's Balsam." The contents of Rösler's dissertation constitute an electrico-physical exegesis on the light of the first day in Genesis 1: 3 in which are blended, in a particular way, the elements of philosophical, scientific and theological interpretation.

Especially noticeable in his interpretation of the light of the first day of Creation as electricity is the comprehensive knowledge of the latest scientific literature used by this candidate of theology. To a great extent, the literature in question had been published only a few years or even months before. It is apparent that the Oetinger circle most diligently collected all new publications in the field of electricity, a practice that certainly necessitates the availability of substantial funds. One of Rösler's main sources was the famous Johann Heinrich Winkler, called the "father of German electricians." [He also consulted] the work of Johann Friedrich Hartmann on the similarity of the electric power to "fearsome Airy phenomena" as well as his treatise on the aurora borealis; he knew the work of Johann Friedrich Mayer and of the Swiss scholar P. W. Ammersin.[27]

Especially noteworthy is his knowledge of Benjamin Franklin's writings–he had a collection of his letters of 1749 at hand–as well as the controversy between French academicians and Franklin and in addition Erhardus Runeberg's investigations of the influence of electricity on plant growth.[28] But he was also aware of clerical essays on electricity; thus he quotes Anton von Balthasar–at the time president of the University in Greifswald–who in his treatise on the observance of Pentecost[29] discusses "spiritual electrisation"–and interprets [as electricity] the Holy Ghost's pentecostal tongues of fire. Adding to this the Oetinger circle's knowledge of Eichmann, Mesmer and Hall, it must be admitted that this small group of "electrical theologians" of the pietistic-theosophical persuasion was abreast with the scientific research of its times and actively contributed to the dissemination and intensification of this research.

[In 1759,] before Rösler's treatise on the light of the first day of Creation had appeared, Johann Kies presented a dissertation on electricity that dealt with the problem of an electrical interpretation of macrocosmic processes, *De cometis et arcenda exinde electricitate ad explicandum systema mundanum a nonnullis advocata* [which sought to "preclude electricity as an explanation for the ordering of the world, which some have advocated"].

Publishing the book on electricity had an unexpected consequence for Oetinger: it aroused the curiosity of Duke Carl Eugen Wurttemberg. The latter had no scientific interest in electricity, but rather was a pyromaniac of somewhat pathological proportions who would personally hurry to places of conflagration whenever there was a fire in the vicinity.[30] Against this pyromaniacal background in the intellectual history of Wurttemberg, a special emphasis is bestowed on the most magnificent poetic description of a fire caused by lightning that can be found in German literature, viz. the famous fire in Schiller's poem "Die Glocke."[31] Duke Carl Eugen felt so enthusiastic about Oetinger's book that he appointed him Prelate of Murrhardt–ignoring the consistory's privilege of making nominations–since a salt mine was located there and the Duke considered best suited for the prelacy a theologian well versed in physics and chemistry. Oetinger himself comments on the appointment in a letter to Count von Castell in 1765:

> His Serene Highness appointed me Prelate of Murrhardt due to the fact that I am a chemist–which he gleaned from my book on Divisch's electricity–because they seem to have found a salt mine there.[32]

In another letter he remarks:

> I have been made a Prelate in a wonderful way *par bricole*. . . In
> a French letter suggested that the Duke might want to consider
> me in connection with the salt mine at Murrhardt. His in-
> formed me that he had already made other plans; three days lat-
> er, he wrote to tell me how grateful he was and awarded me the
> prelacy, telling Reuss that he was appointing me, and no one
> else, because I am a chemist.[33]

It is apparent that the lightning of princely favor did not
strike Oetinger out of a clear sky; rather that Oetinger intentionally
guided the flash of lightning to his house.

NOTES

1. See K. Chr. E. Ehmann, *Ich, Ludwig Fricker* (Stuttgart, 1864), with its bibliography; W. Ludwig, "Neue Handschriften von Iohan Ludwig Fricker," *Blätter für württ. Kirchengesch.* NF 56, (1956): 168ff. [Oetinger also published unedited writings of Fricker in his autobiography,] *Zeugnisse der Schwabenväter,* ed. J. Roessle, vol. V (Metzingen,1903 [?]).

2. [Francis II (1768-1835), the last Holy Roman Emperor, who became emperor of Austria as Francis I (1804-1835). –ED.]

3. Oetinger, *Zeugnisse,* vol. I, p. 90f.

4. Swedenborgs *Irrdische und himmlische Philosophie,* vol. II, p. 251n., cited in Carl A. Auberlen, *Die Theosophie F.C. Oetingers nach ihren Grundzügen* (Tübingen, 1847), p. 11.

5. *Zeugnisse,* vol. 5, p. 10.

6. [(1703-1791). English theologian, evangelist, and founder of Methodism. Oddly, Wesley was also an early experimenter in electricity and had constructed his own machine. –ED.]

7. [(1714-1770). English Methodist revivalist preacher.–ED.]

8. [We have not been able to locate a fuller citation for Nesstfell's "Description of the Copernican Planetary Machine Including an Explanation of Its Uses. . . . " –ED.]

9. "Incomplete but Useful Remnants."

10. See the article by F. Procházka in *Ottuv Slovnik Naučný (Prague),* VI (1893), pp. 666-669; see also J. Priess, Ein Beitrag zur Geschichte der Phy-

sik (Programm Olmütz, 1844).

11. See the article by V. V. Bobynin in *Russkij biograficeskij slovar' Sankt Petersburg*, vol. 16 of repr. ed. (1902), pp. 233-240. Stählin's portrait of Richmann is reproduced in K. Stählin, *Aus den Papieren Jacob Stählins* (Königsberg, 1926), p. 213, with Stählin's legend:

> A Jupiter qui tonne escammota le poudre,
> Lui souffla son éclair et lui pompa sa foudre.
> [From Jupiter the Thunderer he stole away the powder
> Blew out his lightning and sucked up his thunder. –ED.]

Richmann's work, *De indice electricitatis phaenomenis dissertatio*, did not appear util 1758 in the Petersburg Academy's *Nova Acta*, pp. 301-340.

For the references in nn. 10 and 11, I am indebted to my colleague D. Gerhardt, Institute for Slavic Languages and Literature, at the University of Hamburg.

12. In 1753, the year of Richmann's death, Lomonossov published his work *Slovo o jarlenijach vozdyšnych ot električeskoj sili proischodjascich*, together with the Latin version *Oratio de meteoris vi electrica ortis.* They appear in his *Polnoe Sobranie Sočineny* ("Complete Works") (Moscow-Leningrad, 1950-59), vol. III, pp. 15-99. Details concerning his electrical studies are in the commentary, pp. 512-522.

13. Cf. Alfred Rammelmeyer, *Die Philipps-Universität zu Marburg in der russischen Geistesgeschichte*, in *Mittlg. d. Universitäts-bundes Marburg*, A. 2/3 (1957).

14. Lomonossov, *Polnoe Sobranie Sočineny*, vol. X (1957), Letter no. 30 (July 26, 1753), p. 484; relevant commentary is on pp. 316-320.

15. Divisch, *Theorie von der meteorologischen Electricité, welche Er selbst Magiam Naturalem benahmet. . . .* ("Prokop Divisch's . . . long Requested Theory on meteorological Electricity–which he himself called Natural Magic") (Tübingen, 1765), p. 67, pars. 55-56.

16. See Procházka, p. 668. (Citation in n. 10 supra.)

17. Carl Van Doren, *Benjamin Franklin* (New York, 1938), p. 165.

18. *Bolsch. Sov. Enc.*, vol. 14, s.v. "Divisch."

19. A defense against the Church censors' attacks on Divisch is available at the Olmütz State Archives and bears the title, *Crises scripturisticae contra duplicem animam in homine assignatam . . . ab Authore Procopio Divisch S. Ord. Praemonstr. in monasterio penes Znaymam. . . .*(This was made availablet to me thanks to the kind efforts of Library Councillor Dr. Gottfried Mälzer of the Württembergian Landesbibliothek at Stuttgart.)

20. [FRANKLIN.] [D.E.G.] *Dr. Benjamin Franklin's Erweitertes Lehr-*

gebäude der natürlichen Elektrizität, für jedermann fasslich und deutlich dargestelt durch D.E.G. ("Benjamin Franklin's Expanded System of Natural Electricity, Clear[ly] and Comprehensibl[y] Presented for Everyman by D.E.G.") (Vienna, 1790).

21. Tübingen, 1765.

22. Oetinger, *Biblisches Wörterbuch*, ed. J. Hamberger (Stuttgart, 1849), p. 164. This edition does not contain the emblematical articles and offers, in part, a text that is slightly modernized linguistically. A new edition in facsimile of the original edition of the *Biblisch-Emblematischen Wörterbuch* of 1776 was published at Hildesheim in 1969 (*Emblem. Cabinet*, ed. D. Tschizewskij and E. Benz). This passage quoted above can be found in the latter edition on p. 204, in article, "Feuer."

23. Oetinger, Preface to Divisch, *Theorie*, p. 4.

24. *Commentatio Exegeticophysica, qua De Luce Primigenia Genes. 1.3* ("Exegetical and Physical Study concerning the Nature of the Primeval Light in Genesis 1:3 . . . ") (Tübingen, 1764). [In Genesis 1:3: "And God said, Let there be light." In Genesis 1:16, however, "God made two great lights, the greater light to rule the day, and the lesser light to rule the night." What became of the light of Genesis 1:3, the primordial light, posed a problem for theologians that dates back to the time of the Gnostics and forms the basis for the Gnostic light metaphysics, according to which the light fled into matter and has to be redeemed. The electrical theologians took up this question again in the 18th century. –ED.]

25. Rösler here alludes to a reference made to it by Oetinger in his *Philosophie der Alten wiederkommend in der güldenen Zeit* ("The Return of Ancient Philosophy in the Golden Age"), (Frankfurt-Leipzig, 1762), pt. I, p. 181.

26. Ibid.

27. Hartmann, *Ähnlichkeit der Electrischen Kraft mit den erschroeklichen Lufterscheinungen* ("The Similarity of Electrical Power to the Fearsome Airy Phenomena") (Hanover, 1759) and "Vom Nordlicht" ("On the Aurora Borealis"), *Hamburgisches Magazin* 24 (Sept. 16, 1759), 2, IV, pp. 157-160; Mayer, *Chymische Versuche zu näherer Erkaentniss des angelöschten Kalchs, auch der Elastisch- und Electrischen Materie* ("Chemical Experiments Undertaken to Provide Closer Knowledge of Unslaked Lime, also of Elastic and Electrical Matter") (Hanover-Frankfurt, 1764); Ammersin, *De Electricitate propria Lignorum* (Lucerne, 1754).

28. For example, [Abbé Nollet,] "Conjectures sur les causes de l'Electricité des Corps," *Mémoires de l'Acad. Roy. de Sci. à Paris* (1754), p. 14; P. de Lignac, "Lettres a un Amércan, sur l'Histoire naturelle générale et particulière de Monsieur de Buffon," *Abhandl. der Acad. zu Paris* IX, Letter no. II, and X; Erhardus Runeberg, "Abhandlungen über den Einflüss der Elek-

trizität auf des Pflanzenwuchs, *Königl. Schwedischen Akad.* XVIII (1775)

29. *Sacra Pentecostalia* (1745).

30. In Emma Vely, *Herzog Karl von Württemberg und Franziska von Hohenheim* (Stuttgart, 1876), p. 68, we read:

> The people believed that "Charles the Duke" could exorcise fires; whenever he appeared during a fire, people claimed that it became extinguished. . . . For this purpose there were always six teams of horses at the ready in Hohenheim.

During the great Tübingen fire of Sept. 9, 1789, he was said to "provide the most active help"; similarly, concerning the great fire at Göppingeen, we read:

> After arriving, His Serene Highness the Duke did not spare his illustrious person and was present at the conflagration throughout the night.

Franziska, his mistress, always his companion at such occasions,

> her skirt tucked up high, joined the women who formed a bucket chain; both of them neither ate not drank for eighteen hours until the fire was extinguished.

(I am indebted for this reference to Herr Dr. G. Malzer of the Württemberische Landesbibliothek at Stuttgart, now at the University Library at Constance.)

See also Eugen Schneider, *Karl Eugen, Herzog von Württemberg und seine Zeit* (Württembergische Geschichts- und Altertumsverein) (Stuttgart, 1902).

31. Herr Guntram Brummer of Meersburg has pointed out to me that Mörike's poem "Der Feuerreiter" is also connected with the Duke's pyromania.

32. "Briefe an den Grafen von Castell vom Jahr 1765, " in [K. Chr. E. (?)] Ehmann, *Friedrich Christoph Oetingers Leben und Briefe* (Stuttgart, 1859), Letter no. 548, p. 676.

33. "Briefe an den Grafen von Castell vom Jahr," in Ehmann, Letter no. 557, p. 679.

IV

The Electrical Fire of Nature

The new philosophy of life, which Oetinger developed and based on his theory of electricity, has for its point of departure a new interpretation of the story of Creation. This is consonant with his basic understanding of the relationship of biblical revelation to the natural sciences. The divine word of the Holy Bible presents us with the document of the self-revelation of God, who is an *ens manifestativum sui.* This document contains the secrets of nature as well as those of the story of the Life and Sufferings of Christ, since the Lord of Creation and of Christ's Life and Sufferings is the same God, and since the story is aimed at the completion of the Creation.[1] In the story of the Life and Sufferings of Christ a progressive interpretation of the Holy Bible manifests itself which is augmented by the progressive understanding of nature. Thus–on the one hand–the Holy Bible contains references to all hitherto concealed knowledge in the fields of physics, medicine and astronomy; on the other hand, every new insight into nature leads to a deepened unfolding of the universal meaning of divine self-revelation manifested in the Holy Bible.[2]

Oetinger, following Divisch's thoughts, begins with the first chapter of Genesis where we read, "In the beginning God created the heaven and the earth including the waters. Darkness was upon the deep and God created the light." What, then, is this light of the first day of Creation? It cannot be the light of the sun, for according to the same narrative of the Creation the sun was not created until the fourth day. The first light, therefore, has to be something else. At this point the exegete is confronted by two problems which Oetinger defines as follows: "First, what was this light in and by itself and, second, what happened to it after the creation of the light of the sun?"[3]

The answer to the first question already discloses a totally new view of the relationship of life and matter, of spirit, soul and physical properties. The first light of the first day is not a special

45

source of light, as is the sun of the fourth day that constitutes a later stage in the phenomenon of light, but it is rather the electrical fire, which spreads out over chaos as a stimulating, warming and form-giving life principle and, further, penetrates all of matter and, finally, has–as life principle–fused with matter itself. "All conditions considered, the first light is to be seen as nothing else than the natural fire which is justly called a common phenomenon, i.e., an appearance of a light or radiance in the air, in the water, in the earth like a spirit of all created things which this spirit imbues with life and sustains in their strength by means of engendering (springing up)."[4]

In his *Kurzen Auszug,* Fricker makes the following comment:

> There is, however, in the entire world no matter or body in connection with and in which the elctrical fire does not manifest itself in one way or another. This is why our esteemed author ascribes to all corporal entities the electrical fire, to each in a different and individually suited way. . . He is concerned with a higher purpose, viz. to better complement philosophy herself. There are ample grounds, since the elcctrical fire, concealed in all things is the most common and, as it were, the first phenomenon of all of nature whence all its movement, change, etc., take their origin.[5]

This electrical fire of nature, added to matter itself, is the life principle that again and again rushes into new forms, that wants to manifest itself again and again in new living shapes–it is, strictly speaking, the principle of evolution itself that was part of Creation from the beginning and that manifests itself as a principle of "natural creation." An unusually meaningful revolutionary process in modern cosmology! Next to the "first creation" in the genesis through the will of God is placed the "natural creation" whose seed was laid in the lap of matter by God Himself and in which was located the subsequent creation of forms of life. This is the hour of birth of the idea of evolution.[6]

> The first creation which took place by means of God's creative deed was in no need of any other principle and origin than the will of the almighty Creator alone Who produced everything created from nothing; but for the other or natural creation–when God already ceased creating–is needed the *Spiritus mundi* or the light created on the first day which has been proved sufficiently with reasons as well as through the experiments of electrization.

A marginal note identifies the light of the first day as the *Spiritus mundi*–or the electrical fire.[7]

    This constitutes a new view of the relationship of life and matter, of spirit, soul, and physical properties that differs most strongly from the traditional Aristotelean concept of matter as a *nonens*. From the beginning of the world a living life element is added to matter that contains the cause of all future natural creation, an element that Oetinger calls "the electrical fire concealed in all things." The first day of Creation begins in God's adding to, or rather "mingling into" matter this fiery life-element that will bring forth all future forms of life's unfolding. The origin of life is to be sought in the womb of matter itself. "All physical beings have within them spiritual forces which can be stimulated so that they emanate and make themselves known."[8] There is in nature a self-movement that we cannot reproduce: it is in the electrical and elementary fire."[9]

    This also reveals a new conception of the origin of life. Life has already been bestowed on matter as a secret concealed impulse; it lies on what is already there as the *initiator* of all future "unfoldings." Fricker developed his new theory of life especially in connection with the discovery of the bipolar nature of electricity and found in the "circular movement" of electric current a confirmation for natural philosophy's old interpretation of the "Wheel of Birth" that was formulated by Jacob Böhme.

> Only now do we come to the main concepts of nature's characteristics which are to be defined according to the expanded insights into electricity by Herr Divisch. All corporal beings harbor within them spiritual forces, as it were, that can be stimulated so thay they emanate and make themselves known among themselves and to other bodies. In every body there are present those infinitesimal particles or atoms that possess the kind, characteristic, form, and the general shape of the large body to which they inherently belong and in which they find their rest. The universal sages and teachers of nature have through experience found a principle, viz. that everything is in constant inner motion and that, consequently, there exists in all things a beginning or a weak and low grade of life. There are in life, to be sure, forces of an actually different kind, in a certain antagonism and militating against one another, which are bound together by God towards an orderly purpose.[10]

The presence in matter of electrical force is considered proof by Fricker that matter itself "is full of spirit and life."

> Electricity lets us understand that the most subtle and penetrable things lie concealed in the deepest womb of matter, or the impenetrable things. One should like to postulate that Earth is a mother of the very most subtle and thinnest beings and that life is lying at rest in every body. It was Democritus, Newton's precursor, who had exactly this insight. [Baglius (?)], the great Roman physician, concludes with good reason: life is never to be separated from matter, and life or the spiritual parts were incorporated in matter at the exact moment of the atoms' first birth; before that time the nature of matter had been concealed....The *irritability* of matter is also proof of this: for if matter were not full of spirit, it would not be irritable, also no electrical sparks would issue from it.[11]

In these thoughts, the answer to the second question is already anticipated: what happened to this first light when the sun was created on the fourth day? Divisch's answer is this: the first light was sunk into matter itself, it was blended with it, it was enclosed in it. Oetinger formulated this thought as follows:

> I shall now answer the second question: where did the first light disappear to when the sun was created on the fourth day with its own light? After the waters had been separated...and the earth appeared dry and the great light had been created, the almighty Creator squeezed or blended at once–according to the proportions of things–the light into those elements and mixtures–by "light" I mean the natural life–[which] shines and separates day and night *by means of an elastic force,* like a soul or spirit, as the most subtle, fastest, totally penetrating and highest being and universal phenomenon above all bodies, that was needed, when the sun sets. The old universal sages already recognized this spirit of nature–albeit darkly–when some of them gave it the name "elementary fire," others "electrical fire," several called it "primeval" and "spirit of the world." Because they had neither recognized the necessity of electrical experiments for the thorough knowledge of this subject nor had before them the required experiments, they could not yet exactly define what the universal phenomenon of sub-

lunary nature actually was. Now, however, when God has revealed to the world somewhat more openly His miraculous and
astounding secrets of nature–by means of electrical experiments and their science–, we can more exactly measure and
more clearly explain many natural phenomenan which until
now had been concealed.[12]

In [the *De Luce Primigenia*], Rösler says about the first light,

As these matters have already been concealed, it would certainly not be amiss if you should call the primeval light electricity. The characteristic of the subject itself is conducive: God,
"speaking from the shadows, flashed light" (2 Corinthians
IV:6) and comes to meet the theologian intent on the secrets of
nature. The theologian should adore Him who is all the more
majestic for coming to meet us halfway. Precious light,
whence God derived the beginning of Creation and names!
With sunlight He now provides us with natural illumination
and with admiration of Himself. But in the beginning, on the
first day of that first week, when things began to be, He gave
another light, not sunlight. If the sun shines forth magnificently, this light shone forth even more magnificently. Just as
a bridegroom proceeds from his own chamber or from a place
where he had previously been kept (and yet not, as a bridegroom, exuberant before the fact!), God proceeded and rejoiced,
like unto a hero, at the course to be run–rejoiced to show Himself where there was need to show Himself (Psalm XIX.6).[13]

[Oetinger wrote:]

In every body are enclosed the most infinitesimal fiery particles that inherently possess the general shape of the large
body.[14]

Fricker elaborated on these thoughts:

Without the assistance of electrial experiences, the ancients
also recognized that all creatures and natural physical beings
have within them a certain fire. Its origin has been variously
attributed; but what is easier and more understandable than to
seek such fire in the very first being which God by His com-
mand--through which everything is still being sustained--

called forth from the crude, unformed and dark mixture or chaos--for the manner in which the holy men of the Old and New Testament allude to this in their statements; see Isaiah 45.7: I am the Lord, and there is none else...I form the light, and create darkness; and 2 Corinthians 4:6: For God, who commanded the light to shine out of darkness, hath shined in our hearts--and which the Creator after such separation from chaos made into a proper being endowed with form and virtues and giving life to others, viz. the light of the first day.

In its struggle with darkness, such light was gathered together in a certain degree of strength which is far weaker than that of the sun, it was elevated and is, therefore, to be regarded as the first, most universal, purest, most subtle being--appearing before all others and proving itself speedily--that approximates spiritual entities most closely: as such it certainly possessed an elasticity or power of expansion that could, in its strength, cause a strong radiance and that, by means of its speedy motion back and forth, shook, excited and tore away the innermost particles of chaotic matter so that already on the first day everything was penetrated by it and that darkness was expelled.

What is plainer than the fact that the ignited electrical fire possesses these characteristics and causes effects that can only be ascribed to the light of the first day of Creation as the very first element formed out of chaos: it ignites and radiates while the electrostatic machine is made to rotate fast, it can be gathered at a high degree of elastic force in one place, and when it has been gathered there it disperses and evaporates, indeed it momentarily disappears into general nature simply by being touched.

For it is in keeping with constant experience that it lies [enclosed] in all things and that it again blends immediately with the range of the entire physical world wherever it is not made to [remain] in a special state. Does this by itself already solve the problem as to where such first light--which occupied a distant and separate place from darkness and which, as it were, rotated around the earth in a way balanced with the latte--was sent off to by God during the Creation, on the fourth day, of the suns and other radiant or fiery cosmic bodies?[15]

Oetinger apparently makes reference to ideas that he had already encountered while studying the Cabbala and which Divisch took over from him in his *Theorie von der meteorogischen Electricité*, especially the theory of the *Chasmal*. Prokop Divisch writes:

> It is noteworthy that Ezekiel in his important vision of the
> Throne and the glory of God, [Ezekiel 1, 10] observes how the
> most alive beings or Cherubim—who because of their great degree of liveliness do not rest either day or night [Apocalypse
> 4] issue forth from a shining flash of lightning called
> "*Chasmal*" which was initially concealed in a cloud and vortex
> and broke forth through a swirling fire. Such innermost radiance as the purest source of all living, animate and organized
> beings is rendered *"species electri"* by the translators; from
> [this] we may probably infer, first, that the electrical fire is
> really the subtle fiery principle and life-source of things; and,
> second, that it also shows its special effects in the clouds,
> storms and lightning and that, therefore, meteorology is a
> main part of the electrical sciences.[16]

Here Divisch speaks of "translators" who render the word *Chasmal* as *"species electri."* This apparently reflects Oetinger's discussion with Divisch, which can be found in a letter by Oetinger who had an outstanding knowledge of the cabbalistic theory of the *Sephiroth*, or of the "reflections" or "emanations" or "forces" of God. In his letter, Oetinger states:

> . . . I see that you admit no connection of the soul with electrical fire. Indeed, I am not the kind of man who places nature
> over Theology or Scripture. But I do infer from sacred Scripture
> itself, especially in the first chapter of Ezekiel, that the nature
> of the soul is analogous to electrical phenomena. I also cite
> Hypocrites, who derived his principles from tradition. You
> may see that this argument is demonstrated through the Four
> Living Beings in Ezekiel and the Apocalypse, beings which
> are altogether immaterial, since their strength is derived from
> the northern winds, concentrated in a very intense flashing,
> called *Chasmal*. From this *Chasmal* emerge the Four Living
> Beings, souls, intelligence[s]. And these Living Beings are depicted as full of eyes within. In Ezekiel, the eyes are described
> as surrounded by Wheels; in the Apocalypse, however, those
> Wheels constitute the interiors of Living Beings. I should
> hardly have made these conjectures, if they were not substantiated by Scripture.[17]

In a similar way, Oetinger comments on *Chasmal* in his *Theologis ex idea vitae deducta:*

> God does not have gradations. Glory does have gradations
> and modalities, which establishes on His own behalf to be
> communicative and manifestive of Himself. Either God and the
> world are one substance in which the creatures are modalities,
> or He grants modalities for Himself in a manifestation of glory
> which he communicates in unlimited gradations to creation
> not, as it were, from His own essence, but from an abundance
> of freedom. It is not necessary to say, as does Leibnitz, that
> monads are flashes of divinity, for the seven powers of spirits
> are sent forth freely by God–not out of a necessity of exis-
> tence. The Glory of God is primordial and derivative–
> primordial in God and His Throne, derivative in Wheels, ani-
> mals and the whole life of God. Ezekiel says that individuals
> pertain to God as primordial potentialities, prime matter,
> which is born of cloud and fire and passes into a bright flash-
> ing *Chasmal,* whence souls and intelligences have their ori-
> gin--not from their essence, but from the primordial potential-
> ities of God, which constitute rules for the principles of being
> and becoming.[18]

When Oetinger interprets the *Chasmal*–the shining fiery
cloud surrounding the Throne of God in the center of which there is a
"bright light" and from which then step forth the figures of the Sera-
phim (Ezekiel 1: 4 ll]–as the electrical fire, he enters the dangerous
realm of the theory of emanation, in which the difference between the
Creator and the Creation is blurred. If the electrical fire, the purest
source of all living, animate and organized beings, is identical with the
fiery rim of rays that surrounds God's Throne, does this radiance then
constitute part of God's nature, does it belong to his nature, or has it
been "created"? Is the electric fire itself an emanation of God's nature
or is it a created power that was imparted by the Creator to the Creation as a creaturely force?

Oetinger attempted to clarify this question in a way he could
justify as a Christian theology of Creation in that he distinguished between two gradations in "the glory of God"–the "primeval glory of
God" and the "derivative glory of God." The first is the glory in God,
i.e.,the radiant light that is present in Him Himself and His "Throne";
the second is the emanation, the reflection of His glory in the "Life of
God." From the cloud and the fire issue the "primeval potentialities–
potentiae primitivae," and the "prime matter–*materia prima*." The

prime or original matter "merges into–[*transit*]–the brightly flashing [*coruscantissimum*] *Chasmal* of which it is now said that "the intelligences and souls [emerge from] it, not from its essence but rather from the primordial potentialities of God, which impose their rules upon the principles of being and becoming."[19]

It is thus emphasized here that, on the one hand, the intelligences and souls do not emerge from the substance of God and are, therefore, not to be considered a direct emanation [*coruscantia*] of the divine being, while, on the other hand, they are placed in the immediate proximity of the divine being as emanations of His originative potentialities. Thus the "electrical fire," the "balsam of nature,"[20] according to its origin, is not only moved, as an emanation of the primordial potentialities, into the immediate proximity of divine glory, but the aim is alluded to here, the aim of the life force inherent in this fire. It possesses an urge to realization beyond itself that urges to realization at progressively higher levels of being, an urge to evolution that does not rest until life–initially contained in the ground of matter as a primitive force of life, of motion and formation–has realized itself in a physical realm of the spirit in which the will to self-revelation, to a *manifestatio sui* characteristic of the divine being, has reached perfection: "the end of God's works is physical existence."[21]

NOTES

1. See Ernst Benz, "Das pietistiche Erbe der Philosophie des deutschen Idealismus" ("The Pietistic Inheritance in the Philosophy of German Idealism") in *Schelling, Werden und Wirken seines Denkens* (Zürich-Stuttgart, 1955), pp. 29ff.

2. See Benz *Die christliche Kabbala* (" The Christian Cabbala") (Zürich-Stuttgart: 1958), pp. 46ff; [Benz], *Les Sources mystiques de la philosophie romantique allemande* (Paris, Bibl. d'Histoire de la Philosopie, 1968), pp. 66ff. [See *The Mystical Sources of the German Romantic Philosophy*, Allison Park: Pickwick Publications, 1983.]

3. Prokop Divisch, *Theorie von der meteorologischen Electricité*, F. C. Oetinger, tr. and ed. (Tübingen, 1765), p. 2.

4. P. 4.

5. J. L. Fricker, *Kurzur Auszug* ("Brief Excerpt"), p. 71; publ. in *Anhang*

(Appendix) to Divisch, *Theorie von der meteorologischen Electricité*, and provided with consecutive pagination.

6. In regard to the theology of evolution see Benz, *Schöpfungsglaube und Endzeit erwartung* ("Creation Belief and Eschatology") (Munich, 1965); *Evolution and Christian Hope* (New York, 1966; London, 1967).

7. Divisch, *Theorie*; p. 45; see also p. 55.

8. Oetinger, *Biblisch-Emblematischen Wörterbuch* (Hildesheim, 1969), p. 204.

9. Fricker, *Anhang zu der Theoria Electricitatis* [year of publ. not available], in Divisch, *Theorie*, p. 122.

10. *Kurzur Auszug*, p. 85, sects. 20-21.

11. Oetinger, *Anhang zu der Theoria Electricitatis von dem Einfluss... Chemie und Alchemie* ("Appendix to the Theory of Electricity Concerning its Influence in Chemistry and Alchemy") [in Divisch, *Theorie*. –ED], p. 107; partial verbatim repetition in *Bibl. Emblem. Wörterbuch*, p. 203, in article "Feuer."

12. In Divisch, *Theorie*, pp. 4-6.

13. T.F. Rösler, *Commentatio Exegeticophysica, qua De Luca Primigenia Genes. 1.3* ("Exegetical and Physical Study concerning the Nature of the Primeval Light in Genesis 1:3") (Tübingen, 1764), sect. XI, pp. 18, 27.

14. *Bibl.-Emblem. Wörterbuch*, in article, "Feuer," p. 204.

15. *Kurzur Auszug*, p. 73.

16. [Pt.?] 3, p. 100.

17. Oetinger, *Brief an Divisch* ("Letter to Divisch"), quoted by kind permission of the Olmütz State Archives [from] *X Epistola Decani Weinbergensis M. F. C. Oetinger ad Procopium Divisch*, 27 Feb. 1755. Státni vedecká knihovna v Olomouci (CSSR)–M III 28.

18. Oetinger, in his "Theology Inferred from the Form of Life" (Frankfurt-Leipzig, 1765, refers to p. xxvii of Isaac Luria as the source of these cabbalistic speculations. The quotation above is from [Oetinger (?),] *Praeliminaria theologiae* ("Preliminaries of Theology") p. xxxi.

19. In regard to *"Chasmal,"* see also Oetinger, *Anhang*, p. 100.

20. In regard to the "balsam of nature," see Divisch, *Theorie*, pp. 44, 94, 135.

21. *Bibl.-Emblem. Wörterbuch*, in article "Leib," p. 407, "To have physical existence from the flesh and blood of Jesus is the highest perfection, otherwise the abundance of God would not be physically present in Christ. The end of God's works is physical existence, as the City of God clearly demonstrates in Revelation, chapter 20."

V

The New Anthropology

Under the influence of Prokop Divisch's "electrical theology"–which is an outgrowth of the new understanding of the soul-like "electrical fire" already inherent in matter–in Oetinger's writings, even more decisively, there also shows itself a new understanding of man which is equally determined by his new view of the relationship of spirit, soul, and physical existence and which paves the way for the modern holistic understanding of man. Also in the field of anthropology, Oetinger's "electrical theology" overcomes the old scholastic dualism and attains a new position vis-à-vis the contemporary idealism à la Leibniz, on the one hand, and the emerging materialism of La Mettrie on the other.

Scholastic anthropology one-sidedly stressed man's rational faculties. According to traditional anthropology, man is an image of God solely in regard to his ability to think; his creation in the image of God does not extend–as St. Augustine asserts[1]–to man's physical, material, nor even his psychic spheres. On this basis, the total severance of man from the rest of Creation ensued: from both pre- and extra-human realms, especially from that of the animals; thus the consciousness of the intrinsic connection of man with the totality of living beings was destroyed. The one-sided intellectualization of man corresponds to the degradation of animals: with Descartes, in the final stage of this intellectualistic anthropology, animals appear solely as machines guided by impulses of instincts and drives.[2]

Oetinger was motivated to give a new interpretation also of man by the discovery of electricity as the secret fire of nature already admixed with matter. Man is no longer viewed as a being totally severed from the realm of pre-human life forms by the primacy of his intellect, but rather as a being which is involved in all levels of life--the material, vegetable, animal–by means of his soul that has deep roots in pre-human realms. "The first man was made from dust, even so the natural soul was his already concealed in dust. The first forming of man from the dust of the earth was already filled with electrical fire: God did not make a dead human image, but during its formation the machine already received its psychic soul in a concealed manner. Paul therefore says: "The psychic or soul-like was the first, the spiritual the second."[3]

It was in his encounter with Divisch, especially, that Oetinger arrived at this new understanding of man. The clerical censor in Vienna accused Divisch of violating the classical definition in Aristotelean philosophy that formed the basis of Thomistic anthropology: animam rationalem esse formam corporis.[4] In Aristotle matter appears as a non-being, a non-ens, that receives its form from the rational principle of the soul. The soul's rationality, its judiciousness, its ability to impress its form onto the formlessness of matter is declared to be its sole characteristic. Accordingly, the censor reproached Divisch for teaching that the rational soul did not constitute the form of the body.

This reproach, however, is off the mark, as Oetinger correctly observes: Divisch does not intend to deny the power of the rational soul; rather, as a result of the discovery of modern natural science, he intends to state the fact that a dual life finds expression in the soul: not only a conscious and rational but also a vita sensivâ ("sensory, growth-like, sensitive" life). This sensuous soul, however, from which issue order and motion of man's growth processes, the sensory perceptions, and conscious functions of the human organism, is "electrical"; it is nourished by the "electrical fire."

Thus Oetinger answers Divisch's critics:

> There is in man a dual life: that which is sensitive of growth and that which is rational, the former the sustainer of the latter. This, however, does not clearly establish that it is the rational which forms the growth-oriented. The rational [quality of] the soul distinguishes man from the animals, and it is from above; the growth=sensitive, or the psychicum, is from below, as it is with all animals. To be sure, the vegetativo-sensitivum sustains the rational, but the rational, because of this, does not give form to the growth-oriented. The vita sensitiva lies in the organism and in the springs from which comes the electrical fire. Divisch says, "Animal life is formally constituted through the electric balsam of nature and is conserved through the natural electrization of the eyes, of the breath in the throat, and the heat of the blood, and the rational spirit has nothing to do in the body." Accordingly, he believes that the rational has quite a different task, viz. that of

ordering the thoughts, of directing the arbitrary movements. Yet, dear reader, at this point we enter all too deeply into the concealed recesses of the soul. I think that neither Herr Divisch nor any other man can determine to what degree rational life affects sensuous growth-oriented life. This would necessitate totally different experiments [upon] the nature of the soul.[5]

Oetinger repeated this basic thought of his new anthropology innumerable times in his works. This is not a symptom of his dogmatism but rather an expression of the fact that he was well aware of the novelty of his views, of his radical deviation from traditional theological anthropology, and that he considered it necessary to demonstrate again and again his new insights to his contemporaries–who as yet had not recognized the exciting significance of current scientific discoveries for their understanding of man–and to force them to rethink the matter. In addition to giving information regarding the electrical experiments, his announcements of new medical discoveries concerning the relation between mental and organic life–especially functions in the brain, the circulatory system, the glands–serve the same intent: viz. to emphasize the rootedness of man's spiritual life in the organic structures and physico-chemical processes of his bodily existence, and to pave the way to a new theology of physical existence.

Oetinger received his strongest support from Fricker, his student, who in his *Kurzer Auszug* especially stresses Divisch's teaching on the "dual life of man," and who–in a daring violation of the dominant theological anthropology–unequivocally states that man possesses not only a rational but also an "animal" soul.

He [Prokop Divisch] proves that man's natural life--in regard to its sensuous, sensitive as well as growth-oriented quality-- consists solely of the motion in his body of the natural electrical fire which nourishes with its exhaling natural balsam the juice of life, so that man has a psychic, earthly, or animal soul in addition to the lofty light of reason which still manifests itself in part through premonition and correct logical conclusions. So this lesser life sustains itself and spreads farther through a natural, orderly, slow, and imperceptibly progressing electrization: there occurs a certain subtle friction in our sense-organs, notably in the eyes, farther in the throat or larynx for the stimulation of breath and the tongue in keeping with hearing and speech patterns, and finally in the arteries for

The natural soul is from below, from the earth; as the actuating spirit of the human body–and as the opposite of the reintegrating and directing spirit–it has subtle tools, vehicles, and passages in the human body so that not only what happens through the senses but also thinking, talking, and movement can be explained [to some extent mechanically, as the greatest philosophers of our time have made known rather clearly... Since, according to Proverbs 20:27, the soul rules the body by means of many points of light–which are subordinated to each other in a special way–or by means of springs of motion, such triple fire–running from every center *per unam confluxionem, conspirationem et consensum*–is sustained in constant excitation, vibration, and attention so that the life of the animal or soul continues on the right path in sustaining the body without the help of human consciousness and reason and, furthermore, so that in addition to the *motibus volunteriis* all senses and extremities are at the instant command of the ruling thought and predominating will.[7]

In justifying his daring new anthropology, Divisch used the authority of Holy Writ where he had found confirmation for his electrical psychology in the account by Moses of the creation of man. Traditional dogmatic anthropology had understood the act of man's creation described there (Genesis 2:7) to mean that God had shaped an inanimate lump of clay and thereupon breathed into it the living soul: "And the Lord God formed man of the dust of the ground, and breathed into his nostrils the breath of life; and man became a living soul." The earlier fighters for an electrical theology, however, considered it blasphemous to assume that God had created an inanimate lump of clay and, subsequently, had breathed the spirit into it. To them the electrical fire was already inherent in the matter of the clay from which God created man; the lump of clay already possessed a sensitive soul. The breathing-into of spirit is not identical with the act of the first inspiration, but it rather constitutes a subsequent second act: man's endowment with the faculty of thinking, with reason.

Herr Divisch, therefore, professes that the first creation of man from clay happened through the inspiration of the divine spirit in the way in which the animals had risen from the earth, and that God had not first made an inanimate image of man, but that the latter had rather received the spirit of nature during his being formed. . . . And yet it is true that Adam already possessed a higher sensory apparatus of the body, that all men--as they remember in their conscience and heart--can be far superior to themselves and to all natural life due to the assistance of the eternal Word of God, that according to God's determination no solely animalistic man can be called a complete subject, and that reason or the intellect coordinated with the premonitions have a higher origin than the sensory, thinking, and expressive life in the subtle and inner parts of the body, insofar as the latter is not ruled by that Light or Spirit.[8]

In a certain sense, therefore, the hitherto traditional special position of this inspiration [lit.: taking-in] of the spirit is devalued. It is not the first act of inspiration; the endowment with the sensitive soul, with the elastic, formative, fiery, electric force of life precedes it and forms the basis and prerequisite for the transformation through a rational life.

> The first objection is directed against the main idea of his system; the life of the body, it is claimed, must be dependent on the soul, and the natural fire that appears during electrization, on the other hand, is considered to be like unto something inanimate, as are water, air and other elements. The author shows–in the cases of animals, men and plants–that every living body has its tools as special springs of life, since the natural fire works in and through them according to their needs; he also shows from experience that the growth-oriented life of plants as well as the sensory life of animals and men– especially in cases of illnesses of excitations, since nature tends to mend itself–are notably furthered in their regular instincts through electrization; he also shows that certain medicines possess more or less of the electrifiable or passive force of the natural fire, that other medicines possess more or less of the electric or active force of the natural fire and that, therefore, we have to consider only the natural fire–of which medicines partake in certain quantities–the general balsam of life or the supreme tincture.[9]

Oetinger was very careful in finding references in Holy Writ that to him seemed to justify his daring exegesis of the story of Creation and his dethronement of its traditional anthropology. A scriptural passage he frequently quoted in this connection is the statement of Solomon's Preacher (3:18): "For that which befalleth the sons of men befalleth beasts; even one thing befalleth them: as the one dieth, so dieth the other; yea, they have all one breath; so that a man has no preeminence above a beast. . . . All go unto one place; all are of the dust, and all turn to dust again. Who knoweth the spirit of man that goeth upward, and the spirit of the beast that goeth downward to the earth?" Oetinger understood these words, which have a very pessimistic meaning in Ecclesiastes, to indicate a close inner relationship between animal and human life. He sees in these words of Solomon, the preacher of wisdom, a veiled allusion to the community of the electrical fire–now illuminated by the knowledge of electricity–the sensitive soul binding together man and beast, and he interprets this passage as proof of the words of divine revelation for the dual character of the human soul, a character of decisive import.

> It follows from all of this that the natural life of man consists–in regard to its sensuous, sensitive, as well as growth-oriented nature–only in the movement of the electrical fire, which nourishes, with its extraordinary natural balsam, the juice of life so that man possesses a psychic, earthly, sensuous or animal soul in addition to the lofty light of reason that manifests itself in premonition, anticipation, and logical conclusions. The psychic lesser life spreads more and more by means of an imperceptibly progressing electrization. It is notably found in the eyes, the throat, the tongue, and in the arteries for the warming of the blood in that circulation does not take place without friction.
>
> This dual life Solomon in Ecclesiastes 3:18 and 20 distinguished as an animalistic and a higher life. In 5:21 he asks: Who recognizes that the human spirit rises upward and that it has eternity within itself? But the spirit of the beasts goes downward. In man the world is *microcosmic*, as is clearly alluded to in the thirteenth chapter.
>
> As the soul, therefore, rules the body, according to Proverbs 20:27, by means of many points of light that are subordinated to one another in a special way, by means of centers or springs of motion, such fire running forth from every center is sustained in constant excitation so that the animal or soul life continues on the right path--to be sure, without consciousness--in the growing of the body, and so that in addition to the *motibus voluntariis* all senses and extremities are at the in-

stant command of the ruling thought and predominating will.
It is impossible to comprehend this without assuming two
main rulers in the body or without the intellectual and without
the sensuous soul. There exists in man, therefore, a dual life:
the sensitive life and the rational life. The former is electric,
the latter is far beyond electricity, yet the boundary line is impossible to determine. In the reborn man, this spirit of Jesus is
united with the rational life. In regard to the soul, this much
can be deduced from electrical experiments and the Word of
God.[10]

Due to his theory of the dual soul of man, Oetinger is faced
with a difficult problem, the question of the relationship of the sensuous to the rational soul. How is one to view the connection between
the rational soul, which apparently was imbued in man by God only in
a second act of creation, with the already present, fiery, sensitive electrical soul? It was exactly this question to which Oetinger could not
find an answer in Divisch's reflections on electrical theology. At times
he even doubts that there is a solution to the problem. [In discussing
the dual life, he points out that the boundary line between them is impossible to determine.] In spite of this he untiringly attempted to fix
this boundary line in various ways.

At first he believes it necessary to eliminate those opinions
which consider the rational soul a spark, a coruscatio of the divine Being itself. In Oetinger's day, this old theory of mysticism found its
last philosophical expression in Leibniz's monadology, to which Oetinger was totally opposed. The soul is not part of the divine Being itself and does not, therefore, guarantee a natural share of man in the divine Being, but it was rather created in His image by God in an act of
free will. Thus Oetinger writes in his letter to Divisch, "I think, contra
Leibniz, that the soul is not the flashing of divinity; it is not a monad,
as it were, in participation with the divine essence, but is freely constituted by God according to His image."[11] He makes a point of not ob-
scuring the difference between God and man.

But how can the relationship between the "animal" soul and
the "rational" soul be determined in a positive way? Oetinger's most
general expression of this lies in his statement, "If any analogy is to be
made, the electrical fire has always seemed to me to be the vehicle of
the soul, not the soul itself."[12] So the electrical fire is the vehicle of
the soul, not the rational soul itself. In what way, however, the electrical fire can be the vehicle of the rational soul is not clear to him, and
he seeks further instruction on this point from Divisch: "But I could

easily allow myself to be better informed. For this is needed further discussion."

No answer by Divisch can be found to this question. There are, however, in Oetinger's papers, several drafts of an answer which he himself gives to this question. If the electrical fire, the animal soul is the nourishment of the rational soul, then it follows that the rational soul also needs this substratum in order to function. Thoughts also have their physical and organic basis! Again a biblical argument is summoned to support this thought, which was so daring and revolutionary for his times:

> Those Hebrews who think most appropriately according to the model of nature, call such parts of the body as the kidneys "thoughts" as well. Thus David says (Psalm 1:7): "At night, my kidneys discipline and instruct me." In Psalms 26:2, 7:10 he places kidneys and heart together, and Solomon says (Proverbs 23:16), "My kidneys are joyous," i.e., the thoughts that rise from the body. Compare Jeremiah 12:3; Job 38:36; Psalm 51:8. For the thoughts are sustained and nourished along with the physical existence. Thus it is no wonder that one senses and feels one's thoughts; but at all times there is something conclusive in this. In this respect Paul refers to them as enthemeseis ("things in the soul"), because they rise from the *thumos*, from the lower part of the body, and because in its effects the soul is bound to the parts of the body, to the heart, brain and intestines.[13]

Oetinger's view of the direct coherence of the body and the psychic functions is confirmed by the findings of numerous contemporary physiologists and natural scientists. Yet he refuses to explain the connection between the activities of the body and the soul on the basis of Leibniz's theory of preestablished harmony: he considers this theory too external and inspired by an erroneous dualistic understanding of the relationship between spirit and corporeality. That relationship is much closer, more intimate and intrinsic, than was claimed by Leibniz. Thus he also lists Robert Hooke, Christoph Martin Burchard, and, Charles de Bonnet, in addition to Divisch, as witnesses to his new anthropology.

> [The electrical fire] is the principle of all the motions of the microcosm, and the psychic soul characteristic of man is only different in the repect that it is incomprehensibly inherent in

the animal organs and in that it constitutes a sustaining substratum of the spirit or of the rational soul.

And it is this which, in regard to the soul and the electrical
fire, I finally want to touch upon with a few words. Herr Doctor
Divisch points out that the animal soul which we possess in
common with the animals is indeed the electrical fire. There is
much that speaks for this, but it must dwell in the organs.
James contrasts the body with the invisible wheel of becoming and has under it the various fires that belong to the eye,
ear, smell, or taste, as Robert Hooke has shown in his *Posthu-
mis*. The learned Profesor Burchard shares these insights in his
work *Meditationibus de anima* ["Meditations on the Soul"] and
says that it is clear from the effects of the soul that God is immaterial; in spite of this he considers thinking a mixed operation that extends beyond the vital soul in the blood, also the
perceptive soul and mover which is of an aerial and ethereal nature, in reference to which Solomon says that man lives and
dies like the beasts, a statement he would not have made if the
spirit which goes toward God were the causative force in our
senses.[14]

He quotes the same witness in his biblical dictionary in the
article on the soul:

I want to add here the very pronounced opinion of a medical
doctor and professor in Rostock, Christoph Martin Burchard,
from his Latin book *De anima humana*. The effects of the soul
show that there is an incorporeal being within us: but that it is
this alone that executes thinking, is contrary to experience.
During his old age, for example, Newton's efficacy of thinking
was quite diminished: it can also be observed in all of those
who are melancholy that a material being functions in unison
with an immaterial one. Damage to the brain shows the same
thing. Furthermore, during sleep there takes place an inopera-
tiveness of the one principle; dreams testify to the same thing
since they portray all kinds of delusive things in confusion.
Nourishment, warmth, one's way of life considerably alter
one's way of thinking. From all of this may be deduced the fact
that the spirit does not work alone but that it has the cooperation of material auxiliary means in the thinking process. Consequently, thinking is a mixed operation, and it is erroneous to
consider the spirit a thinking being all by itself.[15]

Frequently he also quotes from Charles de Bonnet:

> Bonnet puts before us all kinds of filaments which are sup-
> posed to be helpful to sensations, even absract perceptions. It
> is true, our five senses are in need of filaments and meninges
> for propagation; but if there were no electrical fluid involved,
> there would not be any sensation, there would be no transfor-
> mation of the perceived object. The electrical fire precedes the
> organism. This organic fire of life, this in-flowing spirit, af-
> fects the filaments endowed with feeling. It causes the objects
> to find their way through the filaments into the thinnest of
> spirits, it causes the impulse to affect uniform sensations
> through the disintegration of the particles of light. But no-
> body will explain this completely: we finally have to abide
> with common sense, and in the end we must admit what the dy-
> ing Maupertius said: "We know no more, strictly speaking,
> than the common man."[16]

In spite of this, in other passages of Oetinger's writings the
spirit appears as an element of higher origin.

> It is only the spirit of man that did not lie concealed in the
> chaos, but it must rather be considered an emanation from God
> brought about with the help of the forces residing in God's
> mouth... since it is written that man lives from each and every
> word issuing from the mouth of God.[17]

What a contradiction! On the one hand appear the thoughts
nourished from below, sustained by the vehicle of bodily organs; on
the other hand, thoughts are infused from above, "an emanation from
God brought about with the help of the forces residing in God's
mouth"! The solution to this seeming contradiction must be sought in
Oetinger's distinguishing between two kinds of thoughts: on the one
hand, the thoughts arising from the sensory motions; on the other,
there are the thoughts that enter man from above as an element of separation, issuing from the word of God. Occasionally Oetinger describes
the opposition of these thoughts from below and from above, the
thoughts from the sphere of "irregular inflamation" and the thoughts
from the water of life, as that dramatic struggle in which man's salva-
tion or ruin is decided.

We can clearly sense that the electrical fire participates in all
emotional states, especially in love. Every young man should,
therefore, think things over, when–in wrath or in love–he allows the electrical fire to change into "customary motions"
(*motus consuetudinarios*), since then he can scarcely remain in
a state of freedom unless he defends himself through earnest reflection; thanks to the great persuasive powers of Christ and of
the future world, it is the Christian belief alone that is victorious over these irregular inflammations. Telemachus warns us
of this fire in his seventh book, as does Solomon in verse 5 of
the seventh chapter; cf. chapters 6, 27:28. For according to
the strength with which your spirit is occupied by the lust of
the eyes or the lust of the flesh or boasting, so thoughts will
rise up in you and fill your imagination: consequently the creative and desiring strength of the speaking soul is stimulated
and provides the electrical fire with kindling, either in [the
form of] flattering pleasantness or in an excited bitter vehemence. At this time it is impossible for us to explain how the
elements–which have within them something that is bitter,
sharp, hostile–are separated by the speaking thoughts and how
they are distributed in the blood. Suffice it to say that you
stimulate the quality of that against which you rise up, an in-
flammation of the wheel of nature comes about which is in
constant rotation due to the invisible fire, and this causes a fulminatory electric shock, which is the more noticeable in the
soul as it is very sensitive in the body, and which also shows
its shape in every muscle and membrane. If you do not shatter
the image which acts upon the fire, you are forced to act according to the needs of the body, wherever the excited electrical
fire sweeps you off to. But you are capable of shattering the
image by reflecting upon the consequences or by engaging in
some other elevated meditation. Then you will feel deep inside
you as if you had extinguished the fires of hell with the waters
of life, for James says that the wheel of nature is ignited by
hell, i.e., by the acrid, hot, and sulphuric principles that dwell
in darkness.[18]

Oetinger returns to his distinction between the "thought
from below" and the "thought from above" in his exegesis of Paul.

> Paul separates, as though with a butcher knife, the higher
> thoughts from the lower ones. The Hebrews were correct in
> stating that thoughts were creations, not only as mirror reflec-
> tions but rather through an actual gathering together of their
> elements. . . . The spirit of Jesus is a spirit of order. He who
> has will be given unto, and whoever assembles his thoughts
> according to this order from the words of Jesus, in him works
> and dwells the spirit. The latter separates the passions, the in-
> sidious thoughts, the propensities–from the truth. Those that
> rise from below are corrected by those from above; i.e., accord-
> ing to Hebrews 4: 12, the separation of soul and spirit.[19]

In the final analysis, it is his theory of fire or electricity
which permits him to join together what is opposed. It is exactly the
fiery nature of the sensitive soul which makes it possible for the rational soul to use it as its "vehicle"; it makes possible also that "all
senses and extremities are at the service of all ruling thoughts and predominating wills," for the essence of reason is also fire. But the fire of
reason is also in need of "being strengthened" through the baptism of
fire by the Holy Ghost in order to reach its highest level of understanding. The higher thoughts are not without body. Reason, on its
part, is also only a sustaining substratum and vehicle of the Holy
Ghost, which lifts it to the highest level of understanding and wisdom. "In the reborn, the spirit of Jesus can be united with the understandable."[20] God has revealed Himself in His abundance as the Manifest Being of Himself in Jesus. In His spirit, man attains to wisdom,
which "God infused into the deepest recesses of concealment in matter."[21] In him who has been baptized by the fire of the Holy Ghost, divine wisdom attains to full consciousness of itself. Yet this spirit of
Jesus also is linked to his flesh and blood and possesses also a bodily
transforming power, and the power of transforming into the body of
resurrection, into the state of spiritual corporeality which is "the end
of the works of God."

Thus Oetinger ultimately views the relationship between the
various stages of the soul and their relationship to corporeality as a
progressive or evolutionary series: in the beginning, the electrical fire
that emanates from God as a "derivative force" is infused into the depth
of matter; in the beginning, the higher is admixed with the lower and
"the atoms of the upper air and the upper waters are structured together with the dust. From here the instincts of the animals receive their
form and, furthermore, the lower powers of the human soul.[22] In con-

trast to the monadology of Leibniz--who understood the monad to be a static indivisible point–the soul is "a complex of different forces and essences which initially are tart, fiery, and transitory [and] which in their advancement, however, become sweet, lovely, and firm. The monads are supposed to originate "in an instant"; the soul, on the other hand, "successively." At its final stage or terminus ad quem, it is a spirit [that is also a] corporeally pure being. It extends into a continuum. . . . The soul is a rotating fire that runs its course within itself; it is elevated by a higher light that emanates from the Word of God."[23]

> Purely animal man has no complete being; his nature must be complemented by the Spirit of the Word that was in the Beginning and the spirit of the flesh and blood of Jesus which is a much more subtle being than is imagined by all contemporary monad-poets.[24]

Thus the soul is even incorporated into the process of God's self-revelation which underlies the Creation and the Story of the Life and Sufferings of Christ. The cohesion between the individual stages and levels in the arcane admixture of spirit, soul and body becomes understandable when seen from the end, from the terminus ad quem, from the final stage: in looking back at the points of departure of his electric theology, Oetinger can say from the vantage point of this final stage: "God is fire, my soul is fire, nature is fire,"[25] or, as we could also say: God is electrical, my soul is electrical, nature is electrical.

NOTES

1. *De Trinitate* 1.IX; see also 1.VIII.
2. René Descartes, *Discours de la Méthode V: Ordre de questions de physique* (Paris: Class[iques] Illustr[ées] Vaubourdolle, 1937), pp. 65f., penult. par. Cf.*Theme of Animal-Soul in French Letters from Descartes to La Mettrie* (Oxford, 1940).
3. *Biblisch-Emblematischen Wörterbuch*, repr. (Hildesheim, 1969), p. 401, in article, "Leben"; see also Oetinger's argument, pp. 428ff., in article, "Mensch."
4. In Divisch, *Theorie von der meteorologischen Electricité* (Tübingen, 1765), p. 94, nn. to sect. 27. The fourth item of the second paragraph deals with several objections to Divisch's electrical theories (pp. 94-98).

5. In *Theorie*, pp. 94-95; nn. pp. 94-98.

6. *Vom zweyfachen Leben der Menschen* ("On the Dual Life of Man"), in *Theorie*, p. 89.

7. *"Theorie,"* p. 92f.

8. P. 91f.

9. Fricker, *Kurzer Auszug* (in *Anhang su der Theoria Electricitatis*, in Divisch, *Theorie*), pp. 95f.

10. *Bibl.-Emblem. Wörterbuch*, p. 398, in article, "Leben"; see also Oetinger, in *Theorie*, pp. 46f.

11. *Brief an Divisch* (Weinberg, 27 February 1755). For complete information see supra, Chap. IV, n. 17.

12. *Brief an Divisch.*

13 *Bibl.-Emblem. Wörterbuch*, p. 237, in article "Gedanken."

14. *Anhang*, pp. 162ff.

15. *Bibl.-Emblem. Wörterbuch*, pp. 554f., in article, "Seele."

16. Cf. Albert Lemoine, *Charles de Bonnet* (1850); Herzog von Caraman ("Duke of Caraman"), *Charles de Bonnet, sa Vie et ses Oeuvres* (1859); August Tholuck, *Vermischte Schriften* (1867), pp. 135ff.; Paul Wernle, *Der schweizerische Protestantismus im 18 Jahrhunderts* ("Swiss Protestantism during the 18th Century"), vols. II-III (1924).

17. *Bibl.-Emblem.Wörterbuch*, pp. 247ff., in article, "Feuer": "In the spirit there is something of God that will not perish."

18. *Anhang*, p. 164.

19. *Bibl.-Emblem. Wörterbuch*, p. 238, in article, "Gedanken."

20. P. 400, in article, "Leben."

21. *Anhang*, p. 154.

22. *Bibl.-Emblem. Wörterbuch*. pp. 552ff., in article, "Seele."

23. *"Seele,"* pp. 555f.

24. P. 401, in article, "Leben"; cf. *Theorie*, p. 91.

25. *Bibl.-Emblem. Wörterbuch*, p. 205, in article, "Feuer."

VI

Electricity and Magnetism

Given the state of the sciences during his lifetime, Oetinger can scarcely be expected to have been able to distinguish electrical phenomena closely from those of magnetism. [It was difficult] to tell the differences, when electricity could only be produced in weak currents and was available only at low voltage. Until the discovery of the Leyden jar, the only method of generating electricity was by means of the "electric wand," on which a small electric charge was generated by "rubbing it with hairy cat skins" or "with old winter stockings"; the pioneers of electricity had no clear understanding of the enormous force of atmospheric electricity, otherwise they would not have proceeded so carelessly. Only when such diverse minds as Franz Mesmer and Benjamin Franklin met did the consciousness of the difference between magnetism and electricity gradually develop. This did not, however, prevent the transferral of the philosophic-theological interpretation of the one phenomenon as the basic power in Creation to the other. Oetinger's description of the "electrical fire" as a most subtle fluid of life is scarcely distinguishable from Mesmer's description of animal magnetism. Thus Oetinger sums up the contents of the excerpts he published in his article "*Leben.*"[1] Oetinger himself linked his theory of electricity as "natural balsam" to Mesmer's theory of animal magnetism.

It is a remarkable indication of Oetinger's highly advanced scientific knowledge and of his industry in conducting research that he took cognizance of the latest scientific findings and experiments of European scholars; after all, he only held office in a small town in the Wurttembergian province. Oetinger is the first German scholar of standing who can be shown to have possessed knowledge of the early publications from Mesmer's Viennese period, also a knowledge of the experiments of the Viennese Father Hell, who developed the theory of

magnetism of his teacher Athanasius Kircher to the level of medical
therapy. In his practice, he used magnets in the shape of those physical
organs on which they were intended to have a special effect; thus, for
treating ailments of the heart, a heart-shaped magnet [was used,] etc. In
his article on Life, Oetinger daringly correlated the teachings of Solomon's preacher, the theory on body fluids of Hippocrates, the teachings
of Van Helmont[2] and Jakob Böhme, and the theories of Franz Mesmer
and Father Hell. In Divisch's theory of electricity and Mesmer's and
Hell's theories of animal magnetism, he considered having found a confirmation of the earlier Old Testament teachings of natural philosophy, of the "*physica sacra.*" "As does Solomon in verse 2 of chapter 12,
Hippocrates recognizes three fluids: a solar, a lunar, and an astral one.
The same is quite clear from the latest writing of Herr Mesmer, M.D.,
and from Father Hell's experiments in animal magnetism: and thus
pharmacology receives new findings which are confirmed by Helmont's and Böhme's theories."[3] In this also, [Oetinger and Fricker ap-
pear] to have been the conveyors of the latest magnetic theories and
practices in Vienna.

    While Oetinger in his later works makes no further reference
to Mesmer and may indeed have lost sight of him after the latter left
Vienna, he continued to follow the activities of Father Hell attentive-
ly and again and again refers to him, as e.g. in his article entitled "*Fülle-
Pleroma,*" it is explicit in the context that he spontaneously identifies
the electric phenomena as described by Divisch with the magnetic ones.
In direct connection with the *Theorie von der meteorologischen Electricité,* Oetinger here develops his theory of magnetism.

> Please turn to page 88 in the booklet already referred to, Di-
> visch's Electricité. There you will find that an inner and outer
> nonmechanical agency are collected and put in order for the
> basic formation of things receiving a start in life, an effective-
> ness that calls for a magnetic rather than a mechanical expla-
> nation. With magnets, the following seems to pertain: when
> their substance attracts something from outside of them or re-
> pels it, there exists an internally unnoticeable antagonism of
> two opposed forces, which devour each other, as was pointed
> out in the disputation between H. M. Hellwag and Professor
> Kies, where according to de Tullière and Le Sage, reference is
> made to the mutual devouring of retardation and acceleration.
> From this inner conflict a darkness is born, and from the dark-
> ness a light. This is completely meta-mechanical, and this re-

alization contributes considerably to the insight into the otherwise incomprehensible genesis of the basic formation of man. This will never become totally understood, but every year the magnetic discoveries come closer to the facts. In Vienna, Father Hell has discovered the analogous nature of the magnet to nerve fluid, on the basis of which findings he is curing many patients by using magnetic rings, as these cause constant electrization.[4]

In studying magnetic forces, Oetinger relied on the researches of two additional scholars who in other respects also play an important role in his scientific image of the world: Emanuel Swedenborg and Detlev Cluver. In his reflections on magnetism, he calls upon the natural scientist Swedenborg rather than Swedenborg the visionary. In the field of magnetic studies, Swedenborg was abreast with the scientific research of his times, and he presented a detailed chapter on magnetism in his work *De Principis rerum Naturalium*" ("On the Principles of Natural Things"). Oetinger adopted from this work several thoughts he considered important for his book entitled *Swedenborgs Irrdische und Himmlische Philosophie*.[5] He considers Swedenborg's most important insight his cognition of the analogy that exists between the laws of dynamics governing the microcosm and those pertaining to the magnet.The circular and spiral movements and the vortices of the macrocosm repeat the spiral movements of the magnet. Oetinger incorporated the entire chapter entitled *Von der Ähnlichkeit des Himmels mit dem Magnet*" by Swedenborg into his own book:

Due to their innermost nature, creatures bear a resemblance in their greatest as well as in their smallest aspects. He who understands the smallest, can, therefore, make a similar deduction and comparison in regard to the greatest. Man is in the middle, between the greatest and the smallest: his senses perceive the objects that are equidistant from the greatest and the smallest. He admires that which he sees, he admires that which he does not see: the greatest is beyond his senses, the smallest is beneath his senses. Meanwhile, however, he has a desire to know both. But because he does not know, for this reason he concludes that the created is similar in its greatest and smallest aspects in so far as the innermost forces are concerned.

We behold the magnet and yet do not behold what is in it. So we wonder. In the vibrations of thinking, we grasp onto a firm thought: that there exists in the magnet a likeness of heaven and of earth. There are in the magnet spiral movements, such, therefore, also exist in the heavens. In every spiral movement there is a center, therefore in heaven also. In every rotation around the magnet (*vortice*) motion is faster in the center than it is along the circumference, therefore [is it] also in the circular movements of the heavens. In every wheel around the magnet, the spiral movement is more pronounced in the center; therefore [it is] in heaven also. In the wheel-like motion of the magnet there are atoms that flow around the center and turn around an axis; [so] equally in heaven. The wheel-like motions around the magnet (*vortices*) mutually turn into one another, and in falling one into the other they enlarge the circumference; [so] equally in heaven. Everything is alike, because nature is the same in its small as in its great aspects, especially because the vortices surrounding the magnet have the same atoms as have the vortices in the heavens.

Since, now, man was created to look up sincerely to heaven, and since his soul has been taken from the pure world-air and is, therefore, of divine descent, so we are expected to lift ourselves from earth to heaven and let ourselves be instructed by the magnet-stone as to what is greatest among the visible and among the invisible, and on this basis we are expected, as much as this is possible, to enjoy the heaven in the body; thus shall we learn the beginning of wisdom from our fear of the Lord, which means that our wisdom must have for its goal our veneration of the infinite by the finite.

In this manner we will arrive at the following conclusions:

I. That every element that we have thought of above has an equal effect in the small as it has in the great, in the vortex surrounding the magnet as much as in the vortex surrounding the sun; and as the active center is a movable emanation around the axis, the center of the sun, therefore, is so, too; and that there are innumerable such vortices in the heavens as there are innumerable active centers, or that there are as many suns as there are vortices.

II. That there may exist in the finite universe innumerable starry skies, and that they may be interlaced with one another like the spheres of two magnets.[6]

Oetinger finds confirmation for the same view on the macrocosmic effects of magnetic forces in the writings of Detlev Cluver, who, aside from Newton, is another main witness to his scientific discoveries. Cluver's description of the magnetic force as the hidden basic force in the universe and as the originator of all movement in life shows a noticeable similarity to his own description of electricity as the secret fire of nature:

> This shows that there are certain points in bodies from which light and fire and other central characteristics have their effluence and their influence. This may also serve for an explanation of the attractive force of the magnet. In the magnet, the most subtle force is united with the crudest matter. The divisible force is related to the indivisible point. For into however many pieces one may split the magnet, the pieces will retain the similar points and poles. What is evident in the magnet, seems to inhere unnoticeably in all bodies: they have without doubt their points and poles of for-ces by means of which they react to other bodies, though not all bodies, in consonance with similarly united particles and in dissonance with dissimilar ones.
>
> According to D. Cluver's basic principle, viz. that of an infinite similarity, the structure of the entire world in its greatest and smallest aspects seems to have been secretly formed in consonance with the outward-turned nature of the magnet so that the most subtle aspect manifests its order with the crudest and the crudest, in the most subtle; both together, however, in their respective dissimilarity manifest their similarity in coming from a single container of force.[7]

From this it becomes apparent why Oetinger also interprets Newton's theory of attractive power as a consequence of magnetism. In the entry on the magnet in the index to his work on Swedenborg's philosophy, "Magnetic attraction is the beginning of nature." On the page quoted here, however, he continues:

> In regard to the forces of nature, Newton found in his experiments that it is the attractive power that holds together all of nature, and there this power makes its effects felt far and near *secundum quadrate distantiarium*, according to the distance squared.
>
> In all his writings, Jakob Böhme speaks of this attractive power; as he so often does, he playfully names it, according to the sound of the word, a science, i.e. "something that exerts a pull" (*eine Scienz, das ist eine Ziehenz*). All forces lie undevel-

oped in this first attractive power, which is subsumed in the
self-revelation of God and which is coexistent with His immea-
surableness. The cause, therefore, of this attractive power is to
be sought in the Godhead Himself, not in nature.[8]

Oetinger's relating Newton's theory of attractive power to
Jakob Böhme–indeed, his deriving it from him–does not constitute a
perversion of history by an imaginative theosophist from Swabia, it is
rather in total accord with the historical context: Jakob Böhme in his
theory of the seven powers of God developed the concepts of
"attraction" and "repulsion" in accordance with the cabbalistic theory
of the Sephiroth, the reflected glory of God. The corresponding English terms "attraction" and "repulsion" find their first cosmological
applications in connection with the explanation of the origin of the
universe in the English translation of Jakob Böhme's *Mysterium Magnum*. These terms were adopted from Jakob Böhme's writings and introduced into English by the English disciple of Böhme, the natural
philosopher Henry More. Henry More then became Newton's teacher,
who most strongly influenced his cosmological theories.[9] We must
not overlook or even negate the fact that the language of modern natural sciences and cosmology has its roots in mystical natural philosophy; we must be aware "that knowledge and mystery are of necessity
interrelated."[10]

NOTES

1. *Biblisch-Emblematische Wörterbuch,* repr. (Hildesheim, 1769), p.
398. [See also Fricker, *Vom zweyfachen Leben der Menschen,* in Divisch,
Theorie von der meteorologischen Electricité (Tübingen, 1765).– ED.]
   2. [Joh. Bapt. Van Helmont (1579-1644) was one of the founders of
scientific medicine, who established the connection between chemistry and
biology and medicine. He was greatly influenced by the great physician and
alchemist Paracelsus.–ED.]
   3. *Bibl.-Emblem. Wörterbuch,* p. 399, in article "Leben."
   4. "Leben," p. 229.
   5. "Swedenborg's Terrestrial and Celestial Philosophy" (1765).
   6. Pt. I, p. 7ff.
   7. "Magnetismus nach Detlev Cluver" ("Magnetism according to Detlev

Cluver"), in *Irrdische und Himmlische Philosophie*, pt. II, p. 131.

8. "Magnetismus," p. 108.

9. See Karl Robert Popp, *Jacob Boehme und Isaak Newton, mit Versichnis des englischen Boehme-Übersetzungen seit 1645* ("Jakob Böhme and Isaak Newton, with a Listing of the English Böhme Translations since 1645") (Leipzig, 1935).

10. Paul Hankamer, *Jacob Boehme, Gestalt und Gestaltung* (. . . *"Gestalt and Formation"*) (Bonn, 1924), p. 201.

PROKOP DIVISCH, the other great "electrical theologian" of his day.

VII

Electricity and Healing

Not only did Father Hell and Franz Mesmer make attempts at magnetic healing, not only was Benjamin Franklin interested in the medical application of electricity, but Prokop Divisch already applied his knowledge of electricity as the "life force" with the intention of healing the sick. There are, however, in his extant writings no indications of the healing methods used and of the kinds of illnesses he treated. Several allusions made to Oetinger and the reports of his students Fricker and Rösler on Divisch's method of treating patients, however, show that he proceeded in the direction of the same "magnetic" therapy that was used with great success by his contemporaries in Vienna, the Jesuit Hell and his student Franz Mesmer. Divisch himself refers to his healing method as an "electrization" without, however, "electric shock," as Fricker expressly mentions, i.e., through application of weak continuous currents.

Fricker reports: "Our Doctor Divisch did not make discoveries of a mathematical sort, he searched for ways in which others had preceded him; this is why he was fortunate in curing patients not only without using electrical shock . . . but also in making many new findings in meteorology. To what extent others will make use of this, we will have to leave up to fate."[1] In contrast to the magnetic practices of Hell and Mesmer, Divisch apparently did not use the method of stroking his patients with magnets–Mesmer later reliquished the use of magnets and magnetized only by means of his hands–but rather cured his patients through "insufflation with electrical balsam," during which process, supposedly, after physician and patient were introduced to each other, there occurred a transfer of electric or magnetic force to the patient by breathing on him or by [the physician's] breathing into his nose or mouth, unless the term "blowing on him" (*Anblasen*) is to be understood as a metaphor for the application of weak currents.

The only passage in which Divisch himself mentions his electric cures confirms the proximity of his views and methods to those of

Franz Mesmer. The electrisation of the patient is understood as an infusion with the invigorating natural fire, as an application of an "electric operation" normally performed by nature itself in order to remain in a condition of well-being and good health. It is in this context that Divisch mentions the medical importance of electricity for "the sensitive life (*vita sensitiva*) in a paralytic human being."

If and to what extent Divisch made use of the opposite method also, that of "withdrawing" the "electric fire of nature" from another human being in order to paralyze him in this way "at a distance" as Oetinger claims elsewhere,[2] can neither be proved from Divisch's writings nor confirmed by Fricker. Divisch himself writes about his healing method:

> It has often happened that I cured a paralytic patient through my electrization in half an hour or in a longer span of time due to the characteristics of his condition, something that ordinary medicines could not accomplish. What reasonable and conscientious human being would attribute such quick restoration of the patient to causes other than his electrization--for no other medicines were used during electrization--which loosened his constipation, invigorated his nerve juices and introduced them into the exhausted vessels through transpiration of thickened moisture, and which thereby contracted the relaxation and paralysis? Since diseased and almost deceased limbs receive life from electrization--which is identical with the natural fire--it is logical to conclude that this fire is the life of terrestrial man and not his spiritual soul, especially since the latter has been unable to restore his deceased limbs; therefore the one soul is common to all animals and human beings. It follows from this that living nature must perform in itself an electrical operation as well, however gentle and unnoticeable it may be.[3]

Even though this comment does not facilitate our arriving at an exact understanding of Divisch's therapeutic method, there is at least one thing that can be said with certainty. This is confirmed by the fact that the medical activities of the *theologus electricus* caused great opposition from the circles of medical colleagues. For this reason Divisch felt compelled to include an extensive justification of his medical practice in his writings on meteorological electricity. For one thing, the objections to Divisch were based on ecclesiastical law; beyond that, however, they were inspired by the professional jealousy of the two vocations affected, the physicians and the pharmacists.

Divisch engaged in detailed arguments with both of them. He first disproved the objections that had been raised against him on the basis of the ecclesiastical law's prohibition of medical activities by ordained clergymen:

> The Fourth Objection: Even though this electrical science should retain its rank and advantage in experimental physics, it would still be impermissible for me to conduct the electrical cure and to treat illnesses. First, because the *Sacros Canones* forbid priests to engage in healing. Second, because it is considered contrary to Christian justice to do damage to physicians and pharmacists and to deprive them of their bread.
>
> Irrespective of this, there exists yet another key that allows us to dissolve this main conclusion. First, it is true and quite just that priests be forbidden to engage in healing since due to carelessness a patient is often made worse by medicines, and in such cases disorderliness must be remedied; but the electrical cure is no medicine that is concocted and can be found in pharmacies; it is, also, not dangerous in that it does no harm where it does not also help; and, further, it is not given to the priests by God's church, but rather Christ the Lord Himself ordered them to dispense it: "Go then and heal the sick everywhere." Therefore, it is not downright forbidden to heal the sick, but to do so only by means of medicines that require a special knowledge, which could cause all kind of trouble for a priest because of different dangers that could come up in dispensing medicines. Such contingencies, however, are not to be feared in connection with the electrical cure as long as the one applying electrization knows how to administer the current and to treat the matter correctly.[4]

Equally remarkable is the argument Divisch used in defending himself against the professional jealousy of the physicians and pharmacists.

> ...I can sufficiently justify myself before the other part of the objection raised against me in that the electrical cure does not take the least away from either the medical gentlemen or the pharmacists. For in respect to the physicians, I do not teach that the electrical cure is a downright universal cure, as though one were in need of neither physicians nor pharmacists; in this

regard my judgment is rather that as soon as a person falls ill
he should call in the physician who should examine the state
of the illness and prescribe medicines from the pharmacy; and
if these do not help, he should prescribe others; and if these
also do not help, then finally electrization should be undertak-
en, but definitely not when life is in danger; this procedure can
result neither in disgrace nor in loss for the physician.[5]

Thus Divisch does not intend to deprive competent physicians
and pharmacists of any patients, he rather directs the patients to see the
specialist first. Only when the specialist and the medicines of the phar-
macist fail, does he undertake "electrization." This probably distinguishes him most strongly from Mesmer who was a fierce opponent of
physicians and pharmacists, charging that their art consisted in giving
patients "medicines to the point of killing them"; who wanted, therefore, to eliminate normal treatment by a specialist and instead wanted
to replace it with his own "natural" magnetic practice; and who, above
all, was a grim enemy of "medicines" and thus of the pharmacists.

This may also explain why the highest medical authority in
Vienna appeared as the protector of Prokop Divisch's electrical art of
healing: viz. the Imperial Physician in Ordinary Baron von Swieten, the
omnipotent chairman of the school of medicine at the University of
Vienna.[6]

In his vote for Divisch, von Swieten considered it of decisive
importance that Divisch, in following his priestly vocational conduct-
ed his healing practice by paying due attention to the professional com-
petence of the specialist; this was done in a manner that made inappli-
cable the extant ecclesiastical law's prohibition of practicing medicine.
Divisch writes:

For the protection of my teachings, I will have to quote here
for authoritative support his Excellency Baron von Swieten,
physician in ordinary to His Imperial Royal Apostolic Majesty, outstanding interpreter of the great Börhavius, extraordi-
narily famous man throughout the world. When I wrote this
most learned gentleman, who is favorably disposed toward me,
in regard to the electrical cure stating that some are helped by
it while others are not, and when I asked for instruction on this
point, I received the following kind reply in the matter: First,
the cannon laws of the church prohibit, as is generally known,
the practice of medicine (although not its science) to priests; I
do not see, however, how this prohibition could be so extend-

ed as to include electrisation etc. It is, therefore, permissible to demonstrate what results the electric fire is able to achieve in grave conditions. Second, it should come as no surprise that the electric fire is beneficial to one but not to another in the same condition. The electric force penetrates the entire body suddenly and in a wondrous way and awakens astounding vibrations. It can thus split up bulkiness, move what is stagnating and dissolve that which is constipated and hardened. Where a constipating mass, however, has grown together in the hollow canal in which it is stuck or where it has become diseased, treatment is in vain. Even so, the fact that these electrical attempts have helped many who have undergone them, is magnificent. This highly learned answer in favor of my electric experiments provides me with sufficient reasons to feel that the electric cure does not diminish the reputation of the priesthood.[7]

The most famous Physician in Ordinary von Swieten himself was an "electrical" personage in his time. In a biography dealing with the second half of the eighteenth century, the following statement is made about him:

From one end to the other of the Imperial Royal Hereditary Domain, von Swieten held unlimited sway in the field of the medical sciences. In the center of Vienna University his throne was erected from which lightning constantly flashed down as it does from the throne of Zeus. Stupidity, superstition and charlatanism lay chained at its feet. An iron scepter swayed in the hand of the tyrant. His orders, borne on the wings of the wind, were as impossible to obstruct as are the decrees of the Fates. Thus von Swieten held sway over the school of medicine. . . The medical sciences at Vienna were in the same situation as Russia under Peter I. The great barbarians were lifted to a glorious degree of illumination, but their backs were bleeding from the treatment.[8]

A few years after this opinion was rendered on behalf of Prokop Divisch, on 27 May 1766, Franz Mesmer took his final doctor's examination under the chairmanship of von Swieten and received the degree of Doctor of Medicine from the Vienna school of medicine. The examining board chaired by von Swieten made this entry on his diploma:

We examined him on the entire field of medicine, listened to
the defense of his dissertation on the influence of the planets,
and since he shows a learnedness and knowledge of pharmacology that is excellent in every respect, we gladly award him the
academic degree which he deserves because of his excellent
knowledge.

The diploma is on display in the Justinus-Kerner-Haus at
Weinsberg; suspended from the parchment by a black and yellow cord
is the seal of the university bearing the image of Maria Theresa.

In Divisch's writings, the healing functions of electricity are
also expressed through the characteristic designation of electrical fire
as "the true balsam of nature," a term that Oetinger used often and
readily. This expression already had a previous alchemistic and Rosicrucian tradition but receives new meaning in Oetinger's writings. In
his interpretation of the "light" of the first day of Creation, [Oetinger]
had already characterized the "natural fire" which is "blended . . . into
those elements and mixtures" [of the earth] as "the most subtle, fast-
est, most totally penetrating and highest being and universal phenomenon above all bodies";[9] [Divisch] had shown a direct connection between the modern discovery of the "electric fire" and concepts of the
older natural philosophy and alchemy: "The ancient sages of the world
already recognized this spirit of nature, albeit darkly, which is why
some termed it *ignis elementari[us]* ('elememntary fire'), others, *ignis
electricus*('electrical fire'); a few [called it] *Archaeus* [Paracelsus'
term for the soul-like or psychoid ordering principle of life. –ED.] and
Spiritus Mundi ('Spirit of the World')."[10] It was not until the investigation of electricity that an exact definition of this secret life force,
which had been inexplicable to earlier scholars, became possible.

Because they (the ancient sages of the world) had neither recognized the necessity of electrical experiments for gaining
thorough knowledge of this matter nor had the required experiments in plain sight, they were unable to define with any certainty what the phenomenon *naturae sublunaris universale* actually was. Now, however, that God has revealed somewhat
more closely His miraculous and astounding secrets of nature
through electrical experiments and the scientific knowledge
thereof, one can measure with greater certainty and explain
more clearly many things in nature that had been concealed before.[11]

This understanding of electricity—"since through electrical experience even that which is most concealed in nature has been revealed clearly before our eyes"[12] –also makes possible now the therapeutic application of this "natural fire," which causes and sustains the ordered admixture, movement, electricity, and the right tension in the living organisms; such application is to be made in those cases where the natural harmony has been disturbed; and it is made for the purpose of restoring the disturbed order through the intake of the electricity of life, i.e., the healing of the illness. Thus the "electrical fire" is named the "balsam of nature": on the one hand it is an agent which nature itself uses for the maintenance of the orderly course of life, on the other hand it is an agent used by the "magus" for the restoration of the disturbed order that has come about because of human error and guilt. Divisch traces the term "balsam" to the characteristic balsamic odor that is peculiar to the natural fire.

> The natural or electrical fire always has an odor which, however, is not sulphuric, unpleasant, and unhealthy, but rather especially pleasant and healthy. Until now nobody has been able to give it a name other than the balsamic odor in which the elements are embalmed, the mixtures are made full of life, and in which nature is maintained in its effects, and which it is only fair to call "balsam of nature" without which the earth would be dry and without embellishment.[13]

As Oetinger sees him incorporated in the person of Prokop Divisch, the true "magus" now has the ability of insufflating his patient with this balsam of nature in cases of illness; he has the ability of "blowing it into him" and of "amplifying" in this manner the wearying electrical fire of life that is in the process of expiring. It is characteristic that nowadays we find the purely electrotechnical term "amplifier" first in the context of the physician's therapeutic activities, the amplification of the patient's electric nervous energy: "He, however, who in chemistry and electricity can amplify through iron the true balsam of nature, the electrical fire, and can apply it to the sick without fulminatory force–something the great Divisch achieved–such a person will have attained in the field of electricity an accomplishment that in chemistry is attainable by the alkahest, the ultimate solvent."[14] In place of the dreamed-of goal of alchemy, the finding of the elixir of eternal life, we encounter here the magical power freely to [apply] the balsam of nature, the electrical fire. Again the information is too unclear for us to determine Divisch's exact therapeutic method: the comment that, on the one hand, it is a matter of magnifying the electric fire through iron, while, on the other hand [that] this fire has to be applied to the patient "without fulminatory force," i.e., so that he does not receive an electric shock, seems to suggest that Divisch also used in his treatment weak currents of low voltage, a method that must have been similar to that of Hell, who used actual magnets.

The dissertation by Theophil Friedrich Rösler on the light of the first day of Creation (Genesis 1:3), a dissertation occasioned by Oetinger, contains a surprising amendment to the sparse information mentioned above. Rösler makes mention of Divisch's attributing such a heat and power of warming to the *electrica materia*, that he would only apply to his patients the effluence of this balsamic matter that flowed forth from rods covered with thick wax; he also mentioned that Divisch did not much care for conducting experiments with the Leyden bottle because of their too great vehemence.[15] Since this information is not contained in any of Divisch's own writings, it is probably derived from personal accounts given by Fricker who, after all, assisted Divisch in his cures for months and was well qualified to comment on them to his collaborator in the German translation of Divisch's works. Rösler confirms the already mentioned allusions made by Oetinger and Fricker. Divisch did not care for the method that allowed the crackling electric spark to flash across from the Leyden bottle to the patient; he did not care to administer electrical shocks, he rather seems to have encased the capacitors in wax in order to prevent the spark from flashing across; he attempted to insufflate his patients with the "balsam of nature," the electrical force prevented from discharging.

NOTES

1. J. L. Fricker, *Anhang* ("Appendix") *zu der Theoria Electricitatis* [year of publ. not available], in Prokop Divisch,*Theorie von der meteorologischen Electricité*, F. C. Oetinger, tr. and ed. (Tübingen, 1765), p. 155.

2. *Theorie*, p. 49.

3. P. 39.

4. P. 49.

5. P. 51.

6. Cf. Willibald Müller, *Gerhard von Swieten, biographisches Beitrag zur*

Geschichte der Aufklärung in Österreich (". . . Biographical Contribution to the History of Enlightenment in Austria") (Vienna, 1883).

7. *Theorie*, p. 51.
8. Müller, *Gerhard von Swieten*, p. 34.
9. *Theorie*, p. 4.
10. P. 5f.
11. P. 6.
12. Fricker, *Kurzer Auszug* ("Brief Excerpt"), in *Anhang*, p. 70.
13. *Theorie*, p. 44.
14. In *Anhang*, p. 135.
15. M. Rösler, *Commentatio Exegeticophysica, qua De Luce Primigenia Genes. 1.3* ("Exegetical and Physical Study concerning the Nature of the Primeval Light in Genesis 1:3") (Tübingen, 1764), p. 21.

VIII

Electricity
and
the Last Judgment

Special attention is due the peculiar biblical substantiation that Oetinger, in connection with his interpretation of the Last Judgment, gives for the existence of this arcane life force, which permeates the entire universe, works in every organism and also rules the life of man. The traditional reading of the Last Judgment sees in it the triumph of divine justice--the good are transported to the site of eternal bliss, the evil to hell, the site of eternal torment where the eternal punishment is carried out. The primacy of ethics is so unequivocally predominant in this expectation that the natural-theological aspects of this eschatological drama were totally neglected.

Not so with Oetinger. His theology of corporeality does not permit us suddenly to leave out of consideration the natural-theological, "physical" aspects when viewing the final drama in the story of the Life and Sufferings of Christ. In his view, the *physica sacra* also makes possible an interpretation of the Last Judgment. If the works of God aim at corporeality, then a corporeal-physical process has to correspond to the Last Judgment.

The answer to this question Oetinger finds in a passage from Zechariah, 14:12, in which there is a description of the horrible plague at the time of the establishment of God's Royal Domain, the plague that on this day will visit all of the peoples which have fought against Jerusalem.

This promise describing the punishment of doomsday as a process of total decomposition, which runs counter to the process of Creation, was of the greatest interest to Oetinger. What has to happen in the living organism to enable this peculiar form of divine punishment to take place? Oetinger finds an answer in the newly discovered theory

87

of electricity as the secret fire of life that gives to all living creatures their shape, life, and movement. The enemies of the Kingdom of God are deprived of the secret life force that holds together the organism, allows life to pulsate, and sustains the living form. Atrophy of the electric *balsamum vitae* leads to total decomposition, to rapidly progressing decay of the living body.

Oetinger writes to Divisch: "I am sure that in our time magic has again made it apparent to the pious how this science degenerated because of idolatry. What else is the occurrence in Zechariah but a magical operation by means of which the pious sages punish the enemies of God? I quote the translation of the Hebrew text from Zechariah 14:12:

> And this shall be the plague wherewith the Lord will smite all the people that have fought against Jerusalem: He will make the flesh melt away (*liquefaciendo*), make it atrophy, decay (*tabefaciendo*) (by withdrawing the electrical fire), while a man is standing upon his feet, and his eyes will liquefy--*liquefient*--in their holes, and his tongue will liquefy in his mouth. And it shall come to pass in that day, that a great tumult from the Lord shall be among them. Behold, my discerning friend, how many kinds of magic are enumerated here![1]

Prokop Divisch made this "electrical" explanation of the plague promised by Zechariah on the Day of the Lord part of his book on meteorological electricity. He refers to this biblical example in answering his own question as to where the light of the first day of Creation went after the sun was created on the fourth day. He replies, as has already been mentioned, that God

> imprinted on or admixed with the elements and mixtures (the natural fire), simultaneously as a soul or spirit according to the proportions of things. Where, on the other hand, this natural spirit fades, everything turns incomplete, weak and unable to operate or work. This happens with paralytics and those patients suffering from some kind of paralysis as is the case also in the great plague of Zechariah 14:12 . . . Now, this plague came about because God the Creator and Lord of nature deprived nature of those forces that make up the natural fire (according to the Hebraic version: *auferendo ignem*, through withdrawal of the fire); consequently, the enemies were struck with paralysis, *quasi paralyticis...* [2]

Thus Divisch made a verbatim entry into his book of the excerpts from Oetinger's letter including the latter's explanation of the Hebrew original; in doing so, Divisch mistakenly assumed that the words auferendo ignem were a translation of the Hebrew text, while in reality they represent the "electrical" interpretation of the Hebrew text by Oetinger.

The act of punishment described in Zechariah thus represents the process of decomposition in which the creative act of "mixing" matter and the electrical fire is reversed again: the Last Judgment is the Anti-Creation consisting of the withdrawal of that life force admixed with matter at the very time of Creation.

Fricker once again emphasized this concept in his *Kurzer Auszug aus Herrn Procopius Divischs theoretischer Abhandlung der Electricität* ("Brief Excerpt from Divisch's *Theorie* . . .)[3] the work that Oetinger incorporated in his translation of Prokop Divisch's work.

This interpretation of the Last Judgment as the deprivation of the original life force, of electricity–a concept that closely approximates Mesmer's idea of animal magnetism–recurs in constantly new formulations in the most important writings of Oetinger. Thus, e.g., we also find it in his description of the Golden Age, his description of the impending final stage in the Story of the Life and Sufferings of Christ that contains so many elements of a scientific-utopian and socio-utopian nature. There he describes the judgment of the godless as follows:

> The execution of the judgment on the antichristians will be frightening. It will be the plague on all the people that have fought against Jerusalem (Zechariah 14:12): the electrical fire will be withdrawn from their bodies (a fact already established in some detail by Divisch in Moravia) so that their flesh shall consume away while they stand upon their feet, and their eyes shall consume away in their heads, with which they looked out for injustice, and their tongue shall consume away in their mouth, with which they have blasphemed. And the saints shall go forth, and look upon the carcasses of the men that have transgressed against them. The worm that grows in them shall not die in two or three days, as is usual; their fire shall not be quenched in two or three days; they shall lie as an abhorrence before all flesh for a long time (Isaiah 66:24; Ezekiel 29:9-10).[4]

Despite the similarity that exists between Divisch and Oetinger or Fricker in the interpretation of the Zechariah prophesy, we must not overlook a differentiation that is made in regard to a most meaningful point of interpretation.

With Divisch, it is God alone Who punishes the enemies of His Kingdom through withdrawal of the electrical fire: "Now, the plague manifested itself in that God as Creator and Ruler over nature withdrew from nature those forces of which the natural fire consists." With Oetinger, however, it is a case of the sages performing a demonstration of "magic," i.e., the execution of a magical operation by human beings. Oetinger refers to the quotation from Zechariah in connection with his glorification of Divisch as the true *magus* from the Orient; he sees in the appearance of a *magus* like Divisch proof for the eschatological return of true magic: "I am certain that magic is again revealed to the pious in our time, just as once upon a the time this science decayed because of idolatry. What else is the occurrence in Zechariah but a magical operation by means of which the pious sages punish the enemies of God?" Here it is not God, therefore, but rather the "pious sages" who through their "magical operation" carry out the divine punishment, the withdrawal of the fire of life.

Oetinger gives a similar account in his description of *die güldenen Zeit*: "The electric fire will be withdrawn from their bodies (a fact already established in some detail by Divisch in Moravia)."[5] Here also it is not God but rather human beings who perform this magical operation; Divisch is named as an example of a *magus* who himself has already "established" as a fact that such a magical withdrawal of the electrical fire is a possibility with others. It is apparent that the image of the charismatic human being is here transferred to Prokop Divisch; a charismatic human being is empowered by God to perform acts of punishment and injurious magic.

Divisch himself did not discuss such a case in his *Theorie von der meteorologischen Electricité*. Oetinger alludes to it again in his *Metaphysik aus der Connexion mit der Physik* ("Metaphysics Derived from Its Connection with Physics"): "The great *electricus* Divisch studied the works of God, took Holy Writ for his rule and found that which surpasses all metaphysics. From a distance he withdrew the electrical fire from the body of a human being as a prelude to what we can read in Zechariah 14:12. This is the true metaphysics that offers not only words but effects."[6]

Information on such magical cures performed by Divisch in the sense of working injurious magic can only have their origin in oral reports by Fricker who, it must be remembered, spent several months with Divisch and participated in his therapeutic electric practices. As a matter of fact, in his *Kurzer Auszug*, Fricker himself directly connects the quotation from Zechariah to the "electrical cures." "Thus the lack and deprivation of such an almost spiritual element and natural fire causes either paralysis or death itself, just as the electrical cures sufficiently demonstrate that insufflation with and infusion of such subtle fire restore again to their first life the flesh, limbs and internal organs; whence also derives the punishment of God's enemies, according to the Hebrew text of Zechariah 14:12.[7] Fricker, however, speaks here (with an allusion to Divisch) only of such "electrical cures" during which the patients are administered with the subtle fire–through "insufflation" and "infusion"–for the purpose of healing them; but he does not mention a medical example from Divisch's practice of the opposite case of "deprivation"; he only mentions the prophecy of Zechariah.

NOTES

1. *Brief an Divisch* (Weinberg, 27 February 1755). For complete information see supra, Chap. IV, n. 17.

2. *Theorie von der meteorologischen Electricité*, F.C. Oetinger, tr. and ed. (Tübingen, 1765), p. 4.

3. *Theeorie* p. 5.

4. *Die güldenen Zeit* (1759), in *Sämmtliche Schriften*, ed. K.Chr. Ehmann, vol. 6 (Stuttgart, 1864), p. 23.

5. Ibid.

6. Carl August Auberlen, *Die Theosophie F. C. Oetingers nach ihren Grundzügen* ("The Theosophy of F.C. Oetinger According to Its Basic Structure") (Tübingen, 1847), p. 614.

7. *Die Theosophie*, p. 75; in *Anhang* ("Appendix") to Divisch, *Theorie*.

IX

Magic

When viewing the evolution of the natural sciences in the form of the story of the Life and Sufferings of Christ, all of the aforementioned researchers see a very special significance in the science of electricity. In view of the fact that electricity is considered the secret basic life force, the scientific knowledge of this life force gains a special eschatological meaning. Researchers in the science of electricity typically attempt again and again to attribute to the progress in the electrical science a meaning consonant with the story of the Life and Sufferings of Christ in that they interpret it as the fulfillment of old prophecies. Even the cool, purely scientifically oriented Lomonossov, in his address to the Academy *Ursprung der Meteore aus der elektrischen Kraft–Oratio de Meteoris vi Electra Ortis* ("Origin of Meteorites In the Electric Force"), points out that the discoveries in the field of electricity constitute a science that had been withheld from scholars for many centuries. Lomonossov makes reference to a prophecy found in Seneca's *Questiones Naturales:*

> The nature of things [is that they do] not reveal their secrets all at once. We consider ourselves the initiated, while in reality we have only entered the anteroom. Those secrets do not lie in the streets and are not open to all; they are held back and locked up in the inner sanctum. Many of them are reserved for future centuries, when the memory of us will have long been extinguished, and then our time will look quite different from that which follows us. Great thing come to the fore only hesitatingly, especially when efforts wane.[1]

Lomonossov sees the fulfillment of this prophecy in his time that is characterized by unexpected progress in the field of electricity:

> This significant philosophical oracle has been largely fulfilled

in our time, as the text states, and we admire above all other famous inventions chiefly the electrical force, which surpassed the admiration of all when it ultimately turned out to be a relative of lightning. Those who succeeded in discovering through diligence or through chance the mysteries of nature that had been concealed for so long, have gained a great and unique fame; and it is no lesser fame to have followed in their footsteps.[2]

It is indicative of their importance that reference is also made to the prophecies of Seneca in the dissertation of Theophil Friedrich Rösler written on the "electricity of comets" in 1759.

Reference to the therapeutic application of electricity and the magnet necessitates that we take a closer look at the use of the term "magic," which is so frequently found in this context.

I frequently took the opportunity to discuss magic with our colleague Rothacker. Apparently magic is one of the original forms, if not *the* original form, of priestly activity. It consists of a higher knowledge of the secrets in life's coherence and in the ability to make use of this knowledge with the purpose of intentionally influencing the course of life's continuity. Rothacker reduced this purpose to a brief formula: "The nature of the priest lies in 'helping a matter along'." This may sound a bit anticlerical, as did many things Rothacker said, but it holds exactly true as regards the religious sciences. The priest-magician "helps matters along": when there is no rain, he helps matters along through rain magic so that it does rain; when the buffaloes fail to appear, he helps matters along [by using] hunting magic so that they do appear.

This concept of magic recurs on a higher level of religious consciousness; it undergoes a long process of Christianization that extends through the entire Occidental history of learning. The Christian usage of the term "magic," of the intentional influence on the course of life's continuity based on the knowledge of the concealed life force, is justified because of the basic premise of Christian anthropology which holds that man was created as God's collaborator. Only with this in mind can we make a new differentiation between black and white magic. The good magician works in the name of God and at His command; he collaborates in the building of God's Kingdom.

Goclenius had already given the name "magic" to the central science that grants insight into the secrets of magnetism.[3] Athanasius Kircher also speaks of the *ars magnetica* as the true magic.[4] Insight into the phenomena of electricity and magnetism gave the impression to those scholars, who in the tradition of ancient pansophy had attempted to merge theological with scientific knowledge, that they had finally advanced to the point of understanding the ultimate secrets of life.

In this concept of magic two things are decisively combined: first, the cognitive insight into the secrets of nature and of the story of the Life and Sufferings of Christ. Equally important is the second characteristic of this concept of magic: connected with the cognitive insight into the most secret movements of life is the knowledge of their manipulability, the power to use this knowledge in a practical way. Thus technology also is included in the realm of magic. At this point even the thinkers of that time are faced with the problem of the magician's responsibility to man and nature, a problem that is treated in a way that very clearly distinguishes between an "evil" and a "good" magic, between an epoch of devaluation of magic and an epoch of renewal of magic.

In Oetinger's case the eschatological character of this concept of magic emerges with special clarity. "Magic" itself has its place in the story of the Life and Sufferings of Christ and in the eschatological process of God's self-revelation which is at the heart of all of life's movements. As is already apparent with Johann Valentin and in the Rosicrucian writings, Oetinger is similarly convinced that magic has its place in the original dowry of man–created in the image of God–in the sense of that merger of an insight into the innermost secrets of nature with the control over the powers that are recognized through this look into the essence of all things; Oetinger is convinced that the knowledge of this magic was still extant with the representatives of the initial epochs in the story of the Life and Sufferings of Christ, with the patriarchs, prophets and kings of the Old Testament. It is part of the peculiarty of Oetinger's Old Testamentarian exegesis that he takes it for granted that the patriarchs of the Old Testament had knowledge of the *physica sacra*, of the al*chemia sacra*. This presupposition also makes it possible for him to rediscover the most modern scientific findings of physics, of electricity, of magnetism, even of medicine and physiology in the statements made by the Biblical patriarchs.

But Oetinger also considers the mythologies of the Egyptians and the Greeks evidence of that original magical knowledge whose traces he follows up into the philosophy of the ancients, especially Plato.[5]

In Oetinger's opinion–as already in the view of Jakob Böhme and the Rosicrucians–this magic of the ancients was lost through the fault of people who had turned away from the original knowledge of God and had misused magic for egotistical purposes. The result of this turning away from the divine original image is the fateful separation of scientific and religious knowledge, the loss of that central science in which the knowledge of God's self-revelation in nature and in the story of the Life and Sufferings of Christ was still intricately merged.

The rediscovery of this original wisdom or "Philosophy of Adam" is reserved for the final epoch in the history of mankind, the epoch that will immediately precede the coming of the Kingdom of God. For Oetinger this concept does not have the character of a utopia directed at an unreachable distance but rather the character of an expectation that will be fulfilled in the near future.

He finds the indications for the impending breakthrough of that lost central science which will return in rejuvenated form in the end, of "magic," in the contemporary discoveries of the natural sciences, especially in the field of physics, of medicine and mathematics. He regards his own time–that further develops such astounding discoveries in the various special field of the natural sciences–as a time of preparation for the universal science which will occupy the final phase of the development of mankind in consonance with the story of the Life and Sufferings of Christ, a time, to be sure, that has not attained to ultimate fulfillment. "The time, however, has not yet come when God will remove the veils covering all nations and when Daniel's time of diaspora has ended; only then will we again understand the many kinds of fire that once upon a time God bestowed on man. There is an important reason why God allows them so little to be found now in the meta-mechanical things, in spite of all of the searching done by the scholars of mathematics. Everything is clearly laid down in books, to be sure, but who knows how to gather it together and work on it? Only here can man show whether he is able to fill in the empty spaces and unite the many contradictions of the *Auctorum ex possibilitate naturae*."[6]

Under the influence of his studies of electrical and magnetic phenomena, Oetinger became more and more convinced that he had found the real key to magic, especially in this field of knowledge. To him magic is the knowledge of the secret life forces, of the "natural fire," of electricity that is at work in matter, electricity as the innermost element of life and movement. To him the central object of knowledge is the theory of the electric fire that manifests itself in the innermost recesses of matter as the secret element of movement, organization, and life and that contains the urge for self-realization on higher and higher levels.

Thus Oetinger comments on Divisch's *Theorie von der mete-orologischen Electricité:*[7]

> That is finally the concealed science of magic which in our
> own century but a few people still know because God has al-
> lowed it to become lost until a time when the earth will be uni-
> versally improved. The sages from the Orient knew more than
> we do. The stories of the ancients show that during the times of
> the Egyptians and the Greeks magic was better known than it
> is now. Plato states that magic was [an accumulation] of the
> fire of Prometheus that came from heaven. For the magus or the
> man who studies the intrinsic fire knows how to bring to the
> fore the concealed power of things. He knows that the chaos of
> the inner powers is inexhaustible and that there are . . . mirac-
> ulous things to be brought out, if only one acts according to
> nature.[8]

It is especially this thought that Oetinger expresses in his
very significant letter to Divisch in which he praises him as the true
magician, the rejuvenator of good magic.

In the beginning of the story of the Life and Sufferings of
Christ, the sages–e.g., the patriarchs and the kings, such as David and
Solomon–possessed knowledge of magic that embraced the understanding of the secrets of nature, of the *physica sacra*. This knowledge
was later on lost during the times when the Christian belief and the
sciences degenerated, but it will return in the final epoch, in the time
of the new effusion of the Holy Spirit. In the appearance of scholars
such as Prokop Divisch and Newton and other scientists of his time,
who attempt to bring about a new understanding of the Story of the
Life and Sufferings of Christ and of nature, Oetinger recognizes the
precursors of the rediscovered true magic. Thus he addresses Prokop
Divisch as "You, you who possess a more essential idea of the secrets of
magic *Quis praeter Te id explicabit, qui penitiorem ideam possides ab-
sconditorum Magiae?*" And he continues: "The word 'magic' derives
from the Arabic term *'magash'* which means 'set on fire'. It is you,
therefore, who possess the secrets of igniting, i.e., of magic. There are
evil as well as good magicians. You are a magician from the East, not
an Egyptian conjurer worthy of being whipped. . . . Teach me, and I
shall be grateful to you as a disciple is to his master. I am sure that in
our time magic will again be made known to the pious, just as this
science once upon a time degenerated because of idolatry."[9]

In his *Kurzer Auszug* Fricker describes Divisch's theory of electricity similarly, as the key to all of nature's secrets:

> The author. . . here moves toward the central issue and the bas-
> ic concepts necessary for the researching of the general knowl-
> edge of nature; he expands the electrical insights or the in-
> sights derived from electrical experience and, therefore, guides
> us from the beginning to the point where they can be applied
> to the basic concepts or systems of scholars and where they
> can be used; this is so because through electrical experiences
> even that which is most concealed in nature is clearly revealed
> before our eyes. He, therefore, reminds us initially that neither
> the entire philosophy of Aristotle nor the principles of Leib-
> niz or Newton nor any other knowledge gathered in regard to
> natural things--regardless of whether one approaches them *a*
> *priori* or a *posteriori*, on the bases of chemistry or metallurgy,
> phenomenology or mathematics--will lead us sufficiently di-
> rectly, adequately and clearly on the track toward the *intimis*
> and *minimis* naturae, to the so-called elements about whose
> number even there are so many and various controversies, as
> the electrical experiences and knowledge reveal to us.[10]

In the light of the *Theorie*, magic becomes the "science of the various fires," i.e., the activation of the electrical fire on life's various levels in the universe.

> Magic is the science of the various fires which God conferred
> upon the High Priests for tending and through which they have
> perceived--by means of the divine light--the concealments of
> wisdom which God externally portrayed in His Creation (i.e.,
> the visible things allow a rational perception of God's con-
> cealed invisibilities [Romans 1:20; Proverbs 3:13]).... As the
> Zohar states in Job 11:6, all of magic tends toward multiplica-
> tion, of doubling one and making two out of it; the secrets of
> wisdom, so he intimates, are double that which is, and it is ex-
> actly this that is meant by the Urim and Thummim. In the New
> Testament, too, there occur passages that point to magic: first,
> the one about the Magi from the East; further, the ones about
> Simon Magus and other magicians (Matthew 2:1; Acts of the
> Apostles 8:9, 13:6,8, 19:19). The Magi from the East had God
> for a friend, so that God became what they wanted Him to be,

according to their desire. This is the true magic, and it will return during the final epoch, according to Zechariah 14:12 and 21.21, but it is governed by rules.

In regard to the other wise men, it is certain that no magic can be worked without the assistance of God; but it is often quite mixed up with irrelevant concerns. The devil is powerless without that human being still possessing a ray of the natural light. Through him Satan acts, who rules in the darkness of this world. Otherwise all magic is an exploration of the inner fire, in particular the electrical fire, which is why Divisch called his book *Magia naturalis*. The magician knows that there is an inexhaustible well of forces in nature; he knows how to bring these to the fore, but he needs a vehicle for this by means of which a spirit transfers its impressions to the body; he knows how to bring about other things through their sameness (Exodus 3:2; Judges 1:13,20). The highest magic is the prayer of belief with that love which is formulated in truth. In early times, the charming of snakes by means of potent phrases was a permissible magic Psalms 58:6); yet the uninitiated consider this superstition.[11]

In a similar vein, Oetinger states in his *"Lehrtafel der Prinzessen Antonia* " (Public Monument of Princess Antonia's Teaching Chart"):

I further ask: why does God in His questions descend in such an orderly way from light and darkness down to the very salt of nature?

The answer: this shows that God desires to teach the academies in a methodical manner. From the simple to the compounded, God continues to instruct us as to how hail, ice, and snow--in which coldness predominates--originate, and how thunder, lightning, and diffused and crossed [*durchkreuzte*] out light--in which warmth predominates--originate, and how rain, dew and rime--in which coldness and warmth are balanced--originate, all [being] due to the salt of nature that is generated by the north wind and by the south wind: while the former contracts things, the latter expands them; and thus the circle of nature (Proverbs 3:19, 21) is established. The salt of nature, which Christ so frequently mentions, is in every respect an ex-

traction from the inner fire, by which I mean the electrical fire
and not the burning fire. One has to listen to the greatest electricus, P. Divisch, in this regard.

Why do our current philosophers not want to explore anything in the realm of magic, even though God descends upon
them from light and darkness asking (Job 38:36): Can you in-
troduce reason and wisdom to the concealed recesses of matter?
Can you bestow differentiation upon the power of equation?
.... What, ultimately, is magic? The answer: The science of fire
(in Arabic, the word "magician" means "he lights a fire"),
which raises the *atomos molis* to the level of *atomos spira-
biles*. Then the magician can work with the *ente spirabili* of
Bacon (Baron Verulam. Cf. Sylvam Baconis Cen. X).[12]

In Oetinger's view, the return of magic is directly connected
with the progress in the natural sciences. The further and further
progressing illumination of individual natural domains prepares the
breakthrough of the central science of magic, which will come soon.
Oetinger again and again refers to a peculiar etymology, as, e.g., in his
letter to Prokop Divisch, which plays a role in his interpretation of
magic as the science of the various fires. We find the source of this etymology mentioned again in the article entitled "*Materia*," in Oetinger's emblematic dictionary. There he states, "The words '*magia*' 'magus'
derive from the Arabic term '*magash*' "; Hinkelmann (on p. 118 of his
work *Detectio fundamentalis Boehmiani*) testifies to having found
this in Muhamed Abdel Chalek's *Glossario arabicopersico*, the former stating that the latter explains that the word *magash* means
'burning, lighting a fire.' "[13]

In the final analysis, to Oetinger magic connotes a process by
which all of natural knowledge is raised into the light of divine revelation and by which the natural forces, thus recognized, are made useful for man in the service of God. It is this intention of progressively
raising natural knowledge into the light of intelligence illuminated
by God that he praises in connection with several of his contemporary
natural scientists who, in his opinion, had advanced especially far in
their knowledge, above all Detlev Cluver.

The author [Cluver] postulates that there are three parts to
magic or practical dynamics:
I. To make comprehensible the sensitive parts of extended
matter, or to raise them from the perception of a special subject to the common concept of pure understanding; by doing

this, we anticipate [that] the following [is] to happen: the composition and the disintegration of the faculties inherent in a thing will so be perceived through the similarity of effect and counter-effect that our innermost soul will be transformed into the thing perceived. Thus the magician sets to work using his understanding, and he knows how to make understandable the reasons why that which is at the heart of things is either harmonious or disharmonious; he knows how to explicate this and even how to account for it in regard to the senses, according to Hebrews 11:3. In short, he knows how to lift the mask of that property of a body by which it occupies space and how to gain insight into intelligences and the relationships of forces.

II. The special effect of magic, subordinate to the first, is this: To know the vehicles by means of which a spirit transfers its impressions to a body: to explore how a deceased spirit makes its will known to another and how through its sameness it acts upon another, just as a moving body influences another with the same motion. It should not sound strange to anybody that there are such vehicles, because Holy Writ refers to many of them, Exodus 3:2; Jude 13:20; Kings 19:12; Job 38:1,9).

III. A work of supreme magic is the mental prayer of belief with that love formulated in truth (Colossians 3:2, or to retain God in one's knowledge (Romans 1:28; John 14:23.[14]

This also explains why Oetinger in his letter feels able to praise Divisch as the true magician.

The differentiation between evil and good magic takes on a special meaning for Oetinger in view of the enormous power bestowed by magic. Evil magic uses knowledge for the sake of man's self-elevation in opposition to God and for his elevation over his neighbor in order to enslave him through magic or in order to punish him through performance of magical outrages. It is this egotistical misuse of magic that caused its degeneration and prompted God to withdraw the knowledge of magic from debased mankind. This manifests itself especially in God's depriving man of the command over the magical power of language which had been given unto man as the image of the divine language of Creation: "God prohibited the magical effect of speech even though it did not contain any evil in itself, but rather so that magic will be held in high esteem at the time of [the] improvement [of the world] (Zechariah 14:12)."[15]

In Oetinger's opinion, there were many who exerted the pow-

er of magic in earlier times, although they were unaware of doing so.
Thus he mentions, e.g., the stories of miracle cures during antiquity as
manifestations of performing magic without being aware of it.

For this reason Oetinger in his letter to Divisch adds the following admonition to his praise of Divisch: "Magicians are either evil
or good. You are a magician from the East, not an Egyptian conjurer
worthy of being whipped. I am sure that in our time magic will again
be made known to the pious, just as this science once upon a time degenerated because of idolatry."[16] The rejuvenation in God's spirit will
change magic into a science for "the pious friends of God" who will
participate in the completion of God's works as His collaborators. *Est
magia scientia amicorum Dei, potentiae Dei insistens.*[17]

Of crucial importance in this context is the modernization of
the concept of magic by means of the thought that the new magic of the
final epoch will separate from the "superstititous conjunctions" and
will "set to work using understanding" and will be able to "make understandable the reasons why that which is at the heart of things is either harmonious or disharmonious, will know how to explicate this
and even how to account for it in regard to the senses."[18] With this in
mind, Fricker does not describe Prokop Divisch's *Magia naturalis* simply as a knowledge of the "manipulation of electrization," but rather
as a true pansophy which essentially belongs with a pious, ethical attitude toward life.

> So it has to be clearly stated that this gentleman–who is de-
> pendent on the Lukka monastery near Znaym, who has taken
> the vow of poverty, who in other respects also treats his
> neighbors conscientiously and is willing to serve them–is not
> interested in such a small gain, but rather that he has incurred
> much labor and[many] expenses in his philosophical attempts
> at exploring the nature of the electrical fire by means of such
> experiments; also, that he does not stop at performing the
> mere manipulations of electrization or at observing what can
> be perceived during such experiments, but rather that he has
> penetrated into the entire natural knowledge of the principles
> and main sources of life and all of its movements.[19]

This completes the transition from the old concept of magic
of the magicians and medicine men, of the astrologers and alchemists
to the new ethos of scientific exploration and knowledge. In regard to
Oetinger's view, however, that God had "allowed" this concealed
science of magic in the sense of a pansophy that embraces and unites

scientific and theological knowledge "to become lost until such a time when the common improvement of the earth will take place," we will have to admit that since Oetinger's time the common improvement of the earth has made great strides as far as the advancement of the sciences is concerned; we are, however, still awaiting the reunification of scientific and theological knowledge, which is a prerequisite for the completion of said improvement.

During my last visit to Stuttgart, I was walking down a street when suddenly two boys came rushing out of a backyard: a little boy who was being chased by an older boy. Not only did the older boy appear to be much stronger, but he also held a long wooden sword in his hand. Just before the pursuer had reached his victim, the little boy suddenly turned around, picked up a small piece of wood from the ground, and with the courage of desperation attacked the big boy with the long wooden sword. Brandishing his small piece of wood, he cried, "It's electric, it's electric!" The older boy was so stunned that he dropped his wooden sword and escaped, [running off] into the backyard. Thus I became a witness to the genesis of a myth: the spontaneous creation of the myth of the third Prometheus. Apparently the theology of electricity has deep roots in human nature and in the structure of the Universe.

NOTES

1. M. W. Lomonossov, *Polnoe Sobranie Sočineny* 3, 3 [1950?]: 32.

2. Ibid.

3. *Tractatus de magnetica curatione vulneris* (Marburg, 1609), p. 15: "Magiae dicetur peritus."

4. *Magnes sive de arte magnetica opus tripartum*, 2nd ed. (Coloniae Agrippinae, 1643).

5. In *Swedenborgs irdische und himmlische Philosophie*, vol. II (Frankfurt and Leipzig, 1765), p. 123.

6. In Fricker, *Anhang zu der Theoria Electricititatis*, in Prokop Divisch, *Theorie von der meteorologischen Electricité* (Tübingen, 1765), pp. 152f.

7. In register to *Swedenborgs irdische*, vol. II. pp. 123, 385. See *also Sämmtliche Schriften*, pt. 2, vol. 6 (Reutlingen 1855), p. 378: Register: "Divisch, ein grosser Electricus, macht die Magie klar" ("Divisch, a great *electricus*, explains magic").

8. Register, *Swedenborgs irdische*, p. 123; *Sämmtliche Schriften*, pt. 2, vol. 2, p. 222.

9. *Brief an Divisch* (Weinberg, 27 February 1755). For complete information, see supra, Chap. IV, n. 17.

10. P. 70.

11. Oetinger, *Biblisch-Emblematischen Wörterbuch* (Hildesheim, 1969), pp. 416f.

12. 1763. In *Sämmtliche Schriften*, pt. 2, vol. I, pp. 196f.

13. P. 197.

14. P. 321.

15. *Swedenborgs irdische*, p. 124.

16. See Zechariah 14:12.

17. *Brief an Divisch*.

18. *Est magia scientia amicorum Dei, potentiae Dei insistens. Multi eam exercent nescii. Tacitus de mendicis aegrotis Vespasianum rogantibus ait curatos esse. Quanto magis illi, qui per fidem et amorem primae causae adhaerent, sine multa scientia faciunt similia, vic de magia cogitantes. Sive autem quis hoc nomen intelligat, sive non, quid refert, dummodo vitam Dei sensu intimo pernoscat! Quoties dixit Salvator: Fides te salvum facit!* (Oetinger, *Theologia et idea vitae deducta*, p. 352).

19. *Swedenborgs irdische*, p. 124.